ZIMBABWE @ 40:

Development, Democracy and Transformation

ZIMBABWE @ 40:

Development, Democracy and Transformation

edited

by

LLOYD SACHIKONYE

and

DAVID KAULEMU

Published by
Weaver Press,
Box A1922, Avondale, Harare, Zimbabwe, 2021
<www.weaverpresszimbabwe.com>

and

The International Development Institute (IDI),
59 Mendel Road, Avondale,
Harare, Zimbabwe, 2021

© Each individual chapter the author(s); this collection, IDI and the editors, 2021

Publishing management: Weaver Press
Cover design: Danes Design, Zimbabwe

The publishers would like to express their profound gratitude to the Konrad Adenauer Foundation for their support in the development of this text.

All rights reserved. No part of the publication may be reproduced, stored in a retrieval system or transmitted in any form by any means – electronic, mechanical, photocopying, recording, or otherwise – without the express written permission of the publishers.

ISBN: 978-1-77922-393-7 (p/b)
ISBN: 978-1-77922-394-4 (ePub)
ISBN: 978-1-77922-395-1 (PDF)

Contents

	About the Authors	vii
	Preface	ix
1.	*Introduction: Zimbabwe at 40*	*1*
	LLOYD SACHIKONYE AND DAVID KAULEMU	
2.	*Linking Values, Institutions and Development in Zimbabwe*	*21*
	DAVID KAULEMU	
3.	*Elusive Development, Defective Democracy*	*46*
	LLOYD SACHIKONYE	
4.	*Endowed yet Cursed: Agrarian and mining accumulation in a changing environment*	*78*
	EASTHER CHIGUMIRA AND HAZEL M. KWARAMBA	
5	*Development Aid and the Politics of Development*	*102*
	GEORGE MAPOPE	
6.	*Migration and Economic Development*	*122*
	MEDICINE MASIIWA AND ALOUIS CHILUNJIKA	
7.	*Social Exclusion of Women and Youth*	*141*
	REKOPANTSWE MATE	
8.	*Conclusion*	*171*
	DAVID KAULEMU AND LLOYD SACHIKONYE	

About the Authors

Easther Chigumira holds a PhD in Geography from the University of Oregon, USA. She has extensive experience in both research and development work centred on the nexus of land-environment-livelihoods, agriculture and food systems, climate change and resilience building. Her emerging research interests focus on women empowerment, young people in agricultural commercialisation, and critical thought around black consciousness in agrarian development and land movements.

Alouis Chilunjika is the current Chairperson of the Department of Politics and Public Management at the Midlands State University. A holder of a PhD in Public Management and Governance from the University of Johannesburg, his research interests include public management, public sector corporate governance, economic growth and politics. Dr. Chilunjika has published some articles on corruption, land reform and road tolling.

David Kaulemu (PhD) is the Dean of the School of Education and Leadership and the Director of the Center for Ethics at Arrupe Jesuit University in Harare. Formerly a lecturer for eleven years at the University of Zimbabwe, he currently teaches social, economic and environmental philosophy. Dr. Kaulemu is the author of *Ending Violence in Zimbabwe* (2011) and editor of *Political Participation in Zimbabwe* (2010) and *Imagining Citizenship in Zimbabwe* (2012). His research interests include ethics, social justice, leadership development, conflict and social transformation and Christian social teaching.

Hazel M. Kwaramba (PhD) is a Governance and Sustainable Development specialist with over thirteen years' experience on women and economic empowerment. An International Consultant with work experience in Zimbabwe, Uganda, Ethiopia, Mozambique, Malawi, Zambia, the Netherlands, South Africa and Switzerland, she has advised various organisations on varied dimensions of women empowerment such as African Union Commission – Office of the Special Envoy on Women, Peace and Security; USAID; UNDP; Practical Action; Embassy of the Netherlands; ACE-Europe.

George Mapope is a researcher and public policy scholar who specialises in development consulting. He is the head of Benchmark Consulting, a start-up consulting firm based in Harare, whose work spans the southern African region. His research interests include development economics and policy, political and natural resource governance.

Medicine Masiiwa holds a PhD in Agricultural Economics from University of Rostock, Germany. With over 20 years' experience, he has demonstrated high-level knowledge of international trade issues, migration, economic development and the Diaspora. Formerly a research fellow with the Institute of Development Studies at the University of Zimbabwe, he has provided high-level policy advice, project management and capacity-building services to governments, private sector organisations and Regional Economic Communities (RECs) in Africa.

Rekopantswe Mate (PhD) is a Senior Lecturer in the Sociology Department at the University of Zimbabwe, where she teaches development studies, youth studies and popular culture. She does research on social change and how it affects generational and gender relations. Her publications include journal articles, book chapters and encyclopaedia entries on young people and women in Zimbabwe.

Lloyd Sachikonye is a Professor of Political Science based at the University of Zimbabwe where he has researched and taught for over 30 years. His main research interests relate to democratic processes in Africa and development strategies in southern Africa. Amongst his many publications are *Civil Society, State and Democracy* (1995), *When the State turns on its Citizens* (2011) and *Zimbabwe's Lost Decade* (2012). Prof. Sachikonye is a founding Trustee of the International Development Institute (IDI).

Preface and Acknowledgements

This book has its origins in a project based with the International Development Institute (IDI) entitled 'Zimbabwe at 40'. Conceived in 2019, the project (in pursuance of one of the objectives of IDI) was to 'explore relationships between culture, development and governance processes at local, national and international levels'. In a larger sense, the it offers a celebration of Zimbabwe's 40 years of independence and statehood. *Zimbabwe at 40* therefore explores how the country has navigated development and governance issues since 1980. While four decades is a relatively short period in a nation's life, they were momentous, formative years that should be intensely studied if we are to analyse the present and consider future indicators. What lessons can be learnt from the successes and failures, challenges and opportunities of the last 40 years? What should be avoided in the next 40?

In many respects, this is both a retrospective and introspective book. Conceived by seasoned scholars, it is written from a depth of commitment to an aspiration for a just, peaceful and prosperous Zimbabwe. Most of the contributors are expert researchers in their own fields, which reflect diversity of their intellectual interests. Ultimately, *Zimbabwe at 40* is the product of a team that came together as IDI in 2017 with a vision of a more developed, just and democratic society in which different communities engage one another and live together in peace, co-operation and solidarity.

However, there is a sense in which the project and book represent 'work in progress' reflecting the continuing research, evaluation and policy dialogue that each of the authors in their different areas are engaged with. To that extent, *Zimbabwe at 40* offers a catalyst for more research, more publications while being a contribution to robust, honest, self-critical reflection on national issues. Accompanying the book are extended Monographs that explore in greater depth the themes reflected in the different chapters. The Policy Briefs form yet another output of the project. They engage with policy implications and provide recommendations, and should be read alongside the book. *Zimbabwe at 40* should therefore encourage its readers to explore what is contained in the Monographs and Policy Briefs which may be found on the IDI website.

This project and the publications arising from it would not have been possible without the generous and timely support received from the Konrad Adenaeur Stiftung. We are profoundly grateful for its unstinting support. We are also thankful for the support and co-operation of the team members of IDI and those associate researchers who contributed to the project. Most of the writing of the book occurred during the COVID-19 pandemic with opportunity created out of the adversity of the lockdown in 2020. Finally, we express our gratitude to our publishers at Weaver Press who have been patient and encouraging at every stage of the project.

Lloyd Sachikonye
David Kaulemu

October 2020

1

Introduction
Zimbabwe at 40: development, democracy and transformation

Lloyd Sachikonye and David Kaulemu

1. Introduction

Zimbabwe attained 40 years of independent statehood in 2020. This provides a useful vantage point from which to reflect on the trajectory of its development, and social and political transformation. A time span of four decades may not be a very long stretch in a nation's history, yet for an independent state inaugurated in 1980, these have been momentous decades in laying the foundation stones of development and governance.

While there have been many scholarly studies on how Zimbabwe has evolved over these four decades, there is no unanimity on why the processes of development and democratisation have proved more protracted, formidable and elusive than originally anticipated (Mandaza 1986; Cliffe and Stoneman 1989; Sachikonye 2012). While some analysts (Chipika and Malaba 2017; Mukonori 2012; Moyo, Helliker and Murisa 2008) refer more to historical legacies and colonial origins and restrictions imposed on the post-colonial nation-state, others (Mkandawire 2001) blame the current global relations. Still others (Sachikonye 2012) blame it on political leadership, systems of governance and economic strategies taken by post-colonial leaders. A comprehensive explanation must include all these factors.

Debates have continued over the challenges, and proposals for their resolution, and on the prognosis of the opportunities that ought to be adopted (Bratton 2014; Murisi and Chikweche 2015). These have been framed around various conceptual approaches to development and governance, and strategic policy choices. This book is part of a bigger project initiated by the International Development Institute (IDI) in 2019[1]. The project includes forthcoming thematic Monographs and Policy Briefs.

2. Objectives of the book

This book attempts an insightful review of the experiences that Zimbabwe has undergone during the past four decades, with the hope of drawing salient lessons for theory, policy and practice. These lessons relate to the development and governance nexus, and to challenges, constraints and missed opportunities (Bratton and Masunungure 2011; Raftopoulos 2013; Shumba 2018). Rooted in a deeper understanding of the multifaceted, multi-layered and protracted process of this nexus, the book takes a *longue durée* perspective of the country's trajectory to date.

The broader project on which the book is based seeks:

- to contribute to an analytical review of Zimbabwe's experience in development and governance during the last 40 years, and draw relevant lessons for democracy and social transformation; and
- to research socio-economic development with a view to influencing national debate on key development, governance and transformational issues through public symposia and related forums.

3. Background

The period from 1980 to 2020 spans a number of epochs in Zimbabwe: the liberation and independence transition; reconstruction in the 1980s; neo-liberal adjustment in early 1990s; and globalisation and developmentalism in the 2000s. Like elsewhere in Southern Africa, these processes took particular forms and orientations. Although these were dizzying years during which progress was made on many fronts, regression occurred on others (UNDP 2004) Nothing was preordained. Various options existed, and certain choices that had long-term significance and consequences on

---

1 See IDI, 2019, 'Zimbabwe at 40: development, democracy and transformation', a Project proposal, Harare.

the nature and status of Zimbabwe as a nation-state were made. Decisions made then continue to influence prospects for development, democracy and social transformation. These decisions are ideological, and also influenced by how the political leadership negotiates them.

Consider the conjuncture in 2020. The economy had regressed into a recession with inflation at about 785% in mid-July. Unemployment in formal sector was above 90% (Sachikonye et al. 2018). The proportion of the population living below the poverty line was well above 70%. National domestic and external debt amounted to approximately US$18 billion with arrears rapidly mounting. This economic crisis frustrated official national development plans including ZimAsset, a flagship plan for the period 2013 to 2018 and the Transitional Stabilisation Programme (TSP) of 2018 to 2020 (GoZ 2013, 2018). Occasionally the crisis exploded into strikes and violence as during 2016 and 2019 (PACT 2016; ZHR NGO Forum 2019). A crisis management approach appeared to have been the main mode of economic policy giving rise to uncertainty and unpredictability. Corruption reached endemic levels in both public and private sectors (TIZ 2016, 2018; Auditor General 2019).

Nor were conditions on the governance front much better. Following an interregnum of a Government of National Unity (GNU) between 2009 and 2014 in which a semblance of dialogue and cooperation across the party divide was possible, there was a reversion to polarised politics and intra-party factionalism (Raftopoulos 2013; Sachikonye 2017). The election process remained contested during the 2018 poll leading to opposition claims of rigging and violence in August of that year (ZESN 2018; EU 2018; Motlanthe Commission 2018; ZEC 2019). Efforts to organise a national dialogue have been constrained by the non-participation of the largest opposition party emanating from the narrowness of what is imagined and understood to be national dialogue. The general politicisation of national issues has meant the exclusion of civil society, churches and non-governmental organisations from national dialogue processes.

In addition, various approaches have been advocated with respect to past mass repression during Gukurahundi in the Matabeleland provinces and parts of the Midlands. There is no clarity over which approach and process would allow investigations of what happened and who was responsible, or over issues of justice and restitution. It is clear from this experience that the definition of Zimbabwe as a nation-state is not yet as inclusive as it should be and that the social transformation needed to realise the inclusiveness is yet to happen.

By mid-2020, for economic and political reasons, Zimbabwe was not a settled society at peace with itself. The historical eras cited above cannot be repeated. The windows of opportunity opened after liberation and the Cold War as well as the industrialisation waves of the 1960s to 1980s are perhaps gone forever. Opportunities presented by early globalisation may be disappearing. The global, regional and national environments are seldom static, and it was a weakness of the leadership in Zimbabwe not to have recognised and acted on these realities early on. In reflecting on Zimbabwe at 40, and thinking forward to Zimbabwe at 50, issues of key moments, turning points and windows of opportunity should be explored in structured ways. The contributions in this book point out how the nation can take advantage of these, by:

- Widening the national social imaginary in order to build the foundation of a new inclusive nation and heal the wounds of the past.
- Encouraging an inclusive national development that addresses past injustices and inequalities, especially against women and the youth
- Reaching out to all Zimbabweans in the country and those who have migrated, and to those who have been marginalised, impoverished, ignored and sometimes demonised in order to solicit for their full participation in national development.
- Re-engaging with the international community in order to contribute to the building of a just and prosperous global economic, political, cultural and environmental system that is able to support the aspiration of Zimbabwe's national development.

4. Shifts in discourse: from the 1980s to 2000s

Notably, within a span of 40 years four sets of discourse related to the above-mentioned epochs have animated debate about strategy and policy on development and governance in Zimbabwe. These shifts have had both external and domestic sources and dynamics. They have influenced thinking in policy and academic circles, and also in the media and wider society.

First, during the liberation struggle and independence transition phase, the key discourse related to the link between development theory, capitalism and socialism. Colonialism was viewed as the precursor of underdevelopment. Through suppression of the majority and expropriation of their resources – land and labour amongst others – there occurred enclave development or economic dualism that resulted in the prosperity of a minority of settlers and impoverishment of the majority of subjects (Kanyenze et al. 2011). Defined as underdevelopment, this process was eloquently spelt out in key texts of that era (Frank, 1967; Arrighi 1973; Rodney 1972).

Within the new state elite, socialism was viewed as a key potential pathway to equitable development. Like liberation movements of their era, the Zimbabwean liberation movements subscribed – albeit in varying degrees – to socialism as their ideological framework for the national development progress (Banana 1989). The new state would be a central actor in that process despite the serious crisis that socialism as an ideology and strategy was undergoing from the 1960s to the 1980s. However, the collapse of the socialist economies in the Soviet Union and Eastern Europe by 1989 weakened the socialist paradigm as a rival to capitalism.

Second, with the eclipse of socialism, two major discourses arose to argue for shifts in development policy and governance practice. Firstly, the neo-liberalism that revived and reinforced the argument for capitalist-based development, and inspired the formulation of structural adjustment programmes (SAPs) in most African countries. SAPs entailed sweeping economic reforms to provide incentives to private firms and investors while reducing the role of the state in the economy (GoZ 1991). Having adopted its version of structural adjustment called ESAP in 1990, Zimbabwe soon experienced deindustrialisation and a slow-down, provoking criticism from both labour and capital (Gibbon 1995; ZCTU 1996).

The discourse on economic liberalisation was accompanied by a donor-led insistence on political liberalisation, euphemistically termed 'good governance'. Preconditions for development aid included adopting elements such as constitutional reform, rule of law, regular elections and fixed presidential terms, which partly influenced the outlook of civil society and the fledgling opposition movement (Raftopoulos and Sachikonye 2001; Tengende 2001; Masunungure 2004). This could be said to have had the unintended consequences of causing austerity and inspiring opposition to the government that would culminate in a full-blown crisis at the end of the 1990s. It appeared that the Zimbabwean state and society were not equipped to deal with economic reform challenges and embrace significant democratic reform simultaneously (UNDP 2008). It is a challenge that has not yet been satisfactorily resolved in 2020.

A third discourse related to globalisation, a process that went beyond the confines of Zimbabwe and Southern Africa. It was framed in neo-liberal terms and cast in optimistic tones that implied that every region and country would benefit. They only needed to open up their markets and embrace new technologies. Yet the reality did not confirm this rosy aspiration and outcome; while some regions and countries would have a head start under globalisation, others would be marginalised. As the years went by, globalisation would later encounter some backlash even in capitalist heartlands, yet it would remain dominant as a process and discourse.

Finally, the discourse on the developmental state has been quite influential in some circles, including in Zimbabwe in the 2000s (Edigheji 2010; Kanyenze, Jauch, Kanengoni, Madzwamuse and Muchena, 2017). Initially, a concept closely associated with the rise of Japan and so-called Asian Tigers, it was subsequently extended to explain the meteoric rise of China to an economic superpower status. It pivots on its central role in the developmental process, its functional and symbiotic relationship with the private sector, and massive investments in human capital development (UNECA 2014). Poverty reduction rates have been phenomenal in developmental states like Botswana and Mauritius. It is our observation that this discourse is still playing out in Southern Africa, witness key and frequent reference to its concepts in developmental plans of states including Zimbabwe (Shumba 2018).

Since these various discourses have influenced development thinking in policy and academic circles, there is need to explore their relevance and impact on specific development and governance processes within the broad context of the Zimbabwe at 40 project.

5. Concept and process of development

The concept of development, and the spread of its use, has been traced to the post-war period in the 1940s. It was associated with US President Harry Truman, who used it to distinguish between 'developed' countries (mainly in the West) and 'underdeveloped' ones (largely colonies and ex-colonies in what became known as the Third World). In that context, development was equated with economic growth and a modernisation process that entailed industrialisation, urbanisation and the application of technology.

In contemporary usage, development is primarily associated with economic growth. However, while growth is necessary, it is not a sufficient condition for development. There are instances of growth that have not been accompanied by broad human and social development. Development transcends growth to include the expansion of human capabilities, and social, cultural and political development. Whereas growth relates to market productivity and increases in Gross Domestic Product (GDP), development entails policy interventions to improve the social and political well-being of people.

The evolution of development as a concept includes several landmarks. In the 1990s, the notion of human development encompassed not only income growth but also indicators of health, education and the expansion of human capabilities. This found expression in the Human Development Index (HDI) that sought to measure the richness of human life rather than richness of the economy in which human beings live (Steiner and Dembowski 2020). Another landmark, also in the 1990s, was the notion of sustainable development: that future generations must enjoy the same opportunities as people do today, and that business activity should not damage the natural ecosystems and biodiversity. Sustainable development rests on pillars of social inclusion, environmental protection and the long-term viability of business.

Finally, development requires the removal of major sources of what has been termed un-freedom: poverty and tyranny, poor economic opportunities and systematic social deprivation, neglect of public facilities and infrastructure, and intolerance of repressive states and societies (Sen 1999: 3). In sum, the quality and outcomes of development matter. Yet the inner logic of development to indefinitely increase mass production and consumption can hardly be globalised without provoking future ecological and social crises.

This is the broad framework in which development is conceived and used in this book. It encompasses much more than growth and policies that benefit a few and exclude the majority in society. The chapters are concerned with both quantitative and qualitative aspects of development and how they impinge on issues of public participation, accountability, equality, social inclusion and justice.

6. Development and inequality

There is perhaps no single model for development. Each society, country and continent needs to carve its own path, taking into account what has been done elsewhere, and needs to address inequalities that tend to be inherent in any development process.

In 2018, the richest 10% of Zimbabweans accumulated more income (34% of the total) than the poorest 50% (Makochekanwa et al. 2019). The richest Zimbabwean's wealth was worth US$1.4 billion; the poorest's was worth US$200 million (ibid.). In a country with an estimated GDP of US$18 billion, the total wealth of the 10 richest Zimbabweans was US$4.57 billion, dwarfing the national budget of around US$4 billion.

These statistics still do not convey sufficiently how poverty has increased as wealth for a few has ballooned (ZIMCODD 2019). Extreme poverty rose from 29% in 2018 to 34% in 2019 (World Bank 2019). General poverty has increased to embrace about 70% of the population. Austerity measures in the 1990s and 2000s, and especially since 2018, engendered an enabling environment for inequality to thrive. Budget cuts in public service delivery and new taxes affected the rich and poor disproportionately (ibid.). While some growth was experienced from 2010 to 2014 and 2016 to 2018, this did not reduce inequalities and poverty.

Indeed, a broad trend in regression in development can be discerned in the last two decades. This was reflected in the decline in Zimbabwe's ranking in the UNDP's HDI. Whereas the country ranked 130 in 1998, it slid to 169 in 2010 before edging slightly up to 154 in 2015 (UNDP reports from 1998 to 2019). Its ranking in 2019 was 150, a far cry from 1990 when it was among the top 15 African countries in 'democratic human development'.

7. Thematic focus of the book

The broad purpose of this book is to develop a synthesis of 40 years of knowledge, research and debates about development and governance. The span of 40 years is an advantage in reviewing the broad sweep of policy initiatives, reversals and recalibration in a changing national, regional and international environment. It coincides with the long reign of the country's founding father, Robert Mugabe, who was president until ousted in 2017, and subsequently died in 2019.

What broad lessons can be drawn from how development and

governance have been conceived, implemented and evaluated over the past 40 years? The debate about lessons (or lack of them) includes consideration of legacies of liberation movement, about the party-state and its tendencies as well as about the ideologies that motivated them. Ultimately, this book is both retrospective and prospective. For instance, what is the significance of the experiences of the past four decades for the development and governance choices in the next ten years? Is the goal of an upper- middle-income society in Zimbabwe by 2030 a realistic one? What other visions could be relevant and resonant? These are key questions that guide our thematic focus in this project and book.

7.1 Values, identities, dialogue and social imaginary

The impasse in Zimbabwe should not be viewed as strictly, or even largely, a development question. It is an issue that is interconnected to the embedded history, culture and values of the society. Unsettled questions relate to historical and contemporary experiences of discrimination and marginalisation on the basis of identity, ethnicity, region, gender, age, party and religion (CCJPZ and LRF 1997; Alexander et al. 2000; Reeler 2017). Victims of past pogroms such as Gukurahundi seek truth, justice and healing from events of 40 years ago before meaningful closure is possible.

In a broad sense, Zimbabwe stands at a crossroads. There is a national yearning to move from a painful past and present to a better socio-economic and governance condition. The major challenge is to figure out how to preserve the gains from the liberation struggle in a new social milieu of sustainable development, rule of law and democracy (Kaulemu 2019).

Following this Introductory chapter, the second chapter by David Kaulemu explores the relationships and dynamics between culture, traditions, values and institutional structures that shape development in Zimbabwe. It tracks in broad terms the values influencing visions and practices of development since independence. Kaulemu argues that the values that we need as a nation must be able to take each section of Zimbabwean society beyond its 'common sense', and its naïve consciousness and comfort zone in order to expand its imagined sense of community to embrace other communities that have invested their lives and resources in the country.

A related argument posed in the chapter is that the lack of a shared social imaginary that is consistent with democratic practice and informs our social engagement was at the centre of Zimbabwe's multiple crises.

The widening of an imagined Zimbabwean community was critically important for governance and development. This should be addressed by the cultivation, widening and deepening of a national social imaginary that is consistent with social justice, integration and cohesion at all levels of society.

The chapter observes that Zimbabwe at 40 finds itself in a Gramscian interregnum in which old ways no longer work, and new ways are not yet invented and articulated. The current impasse is a clear indication of the failure of Zimbabwe's population and major economic and political forces to make a decisive move on this issue.

7.2 Elusive development and defective democracy

As we reflect over the past 40 years, the compelling question is why Zimbabwe's pace of development has been so slow that it has lagged behind its neighbours such as Botswana, Namibia and South Africa despite its rich endowments of both human and natural resources. There have been times (for example between 2000 and 2008) during which economic contraction was significant, and periods of shocks (between 2017 and 2019). What explains Zimbabwe's exceptionality in development slowdown and stagnation? Some would explain it in terms of the autocratic political leadership symbolised by the long reign of Robert Mugabe (Mandaza and Peterson 2015; Simpson and Hawkins 2018). Others would identify the cause in systemic failure: the combination of resilient authoritarianism, extractive institutions and absence of a developmental coalition (Bratton and Masunungure 2011). Still others would pin the main factor as sanctions applied against the Mugabe administration by the West from 2002. This project seeks to assess these perspectives and assessments, and weave a more coherent analytical explanation for the country's development performance.

Part of the search for the causes of development stagnation, recession and weak recovery relates to the management of what has been termed the development-governance nexus. The third chapter by Lloyd Sachikonye seeks to explore why the politics of 'resilient authoritarianism' has nurtured conditions of enormous concentration of power in the party-state to the detriment of accountability and transparency in governance resulting in unchecked corruption and significant misappropriation of public resources that should have been invested in development (Bratton 2014). The concentration rather than dispersal of power entailed the frustration of both entrepreneurship, and the growth of vibrant business sectors (Masiyiwa 2016). The growth of a predatory state enabled the spread of cartels linked to the state that were inefficient and corrupt in their tendencies (Shumba 2018). Consequently, the mode of accumulation during the greater part of the four decades was not dynamic, efficient and inclusive. Concentration of power, the existence of party-linked cartels and slow growth abetted factionalism as a form of competition for limited state resources culminating in a coup in 2017.

The chapter explores in considerable detail the notable development experiences in the 1980s that were hailed for the stability they provided to the new state. However, the second decade would witness reverses, especially in social development fields of education and health, partly as a consequence of structural adjustment and economic slowdown. The next two decades would endure severe contraction between 2000 and 2008, and economic turbulence between 2014 and 2020. Periods of contraction and turbulence coincided with political crises. The chapter illustrates the development-governance nexus by showing how trends towards patronage, corruption and institutional decay deepened between 2000 and 2020.

7.3 Natural resource endowments and development

A defining moment in the post-colonial period was the issue of land distribution in a context of extreme inequality in ownership and control (Utete Report 2003; Scoones, Marongwe, Mavedzenge, J. Mahenehene, F. Murimbarimba and C. Sukume 2010; Moyo and Chambati 2013). In addition to land, other key natural resources include coal, platinum, gold, diamonds, chrome, copper and lithium. However, the abundance of these has not necessarily translated into rapid development, and a transition to industrialisation.

Debates continue over whether resource abundance might not have turned into a resource curse. Massive leakages through smuggling and illicit transfer pricing have cancelled out potential benefits from exploiting natural resources (Saunders and Nyamunda 2016). Furthermore, conflicts over access to minerals such as gold and diamonds have spilled over into intermittent violence over the past ten years. Some of the key issues under this theme explore whether such concepts as 'resource nationalism' and 'resource curse' fully explain the economic and political patterns and ramifications of these conflicts.

In their chapter, Easther Chigumira and Hazel Kwaramba seek to unpack

Zimbabwe's development pathway with a particular focus on land and mineral rights. Despite extensive mineral endowments and comprehensive land reform, substantial development had not yet resulted forty years on. The chapter reflects on the fact that the decade of land reform in the 2000s was also marked by economic and political crises. It was a decade that witnessed convulsions in which new social relations emerged, and the state was reconfigured in a more authoritarian fashion.

However, notable post-land reform achievements included more equitable land redistribution and growth in tobacco production and exports by small farmers. Chigumira and Kwaramba argue that land reform signified the final process in Zimbabwe's decolonisation. The proliferation of artisanal small-scale mining, especially of gold and diamonds, became a key feature of accumulation, although state authorities continued to regulate and push back the small miners in major mining zones.

The chapter observes that a debate continues in the literature between a positive appraisal of the land reform and indigenisation processes, and a more critical evaluation. In the context of the prolonged economic crisis faced by the country, the critique that argues that the redistributive programme that sought to 're-peasantise' formerly large-scale farms has resulted in lower production, poverty increase and challenges in production financing, cannot be dismissed out of hand. Persistent land-related and mining conflicts reflect a 'curse' rather than blessed 'endowments'. As other chapters concur, the land and mining sectors have not been spared the rent-seeking, corruption and elite capture.

7.4 Development aid and the politics of development

In our review of Zimbabwe's past four decades, the looming significance of foreign aid since 1980 is central to explaining the trajectory of the economy and social policies, particularly those pertaining to poverty reduction. Foreign aid consists of grants, humanitarian assistance and technical aid in the form of educational, health and related forms of assistance. What have been the predominant forms of such foreign assistance, and to what degree has it contributed to the development process? To what extent, if any, has it contributed to dependency on the part of the Zimbabwe state and local communities, and with what consequences for the conception and practice of development?

These questions are all the more relevant given the gap that exists in studies about the patterns and impact of foreign aid in the past forty years. Such aid has different sources – bilateral and multilateral – and its modalities and outcomes vary widely. The synergies between varieties of aid need to be explored to deepen our understanding, and set an agenda for rethinking foreign aid, poverty reduction and social policy strategies.

The chapter by George Mapope examines flows of development aid since 1980, tracing the years of bounty and diminishing aid, and the factors contributing to its peaks and decline. This is an area that has received little attention, despite its significance. Mapope begins by observing that the ultimate objective of aid for donor states and agencies is to use it as a foreign policy tool, to catalyse trade and enhance access to extractive resources. Tracing the flows of aid over the decades, the chapter notes that a steady increase in the 1980s and 1990s was followed by decline after 2000 owing to strained relations with the West, and the imposition of targeted restrictive measures described as sanctions. The economic crisis in the 2000s was exacerbated by restriction of access to grants and loans as well as balance of payments support from international financial institutions. Those restrictions have continued despite pleas for their relaxation.

The chapter also observes that the administration of development and humanitarian assistance has been affected by the spread of corruption, particularly since 2000. It is argued that development aid is rife with a lack of accountability rendering it fungible by corrupt politicians and officials. In such instances, assistance is exploited as political capital at the cost of national development and welfare. Mapope concludes by showing the relevance of the politics of development to how resources are produced, distributed and used; and for the capacity of the Zimbabwean state in managing development and humanitarian aid.

7.5 Migration and economic development

In 1980, Zimbabwe had one of the best economic development prospects in Africa, as we observed above. It had a diversified manufacturing sector fuelled by a thriving agricultural base. Four decades later, Zimbabwe's economy is reeling under severe challenges, typified by deindustrialisation, debt burden, high unemployment, brain drain and the informalisation of the economy. Hardly 10% of the workforce is employed in the formal sector. The decline in the economy has been attributed in part to lack of investment, unstable commodity prices, climate change-induced droughts, corruption and poor policy choices.

Taking into account that up to three million Zimbabweans that have migrated in the past two decades, the project will explore policy responses that Zimbabwe should adopt to optimise the participation of the Diaspora in national development (Masiiwa 2019). Experiences from other developing countries – including Ghana, Ethiopia, India and China – provide ample evidence of how Diaspora investments and remittances positively contribute to a country's resources and spur growth.

The contribution of migration to economic and social development is explored in the chapter my Medicine Masiiwa and Alouis Chilunjika. Focusing largely on international migration, the chapter defines two main phases, first in the 1980s dominated by white emigration, and second from the late 1990s to the present. They see the second wave as more diverse, ranging from unskilled and irregular migrants to skilled and professional migrants. While noting that migration has also extended to Europe, the Americas and Australasia, their chapter focuses on migrants in Southern African countries, principally Botswana, South Africa and Zambia.

Masiiwa and Chilunjika explore the triggers of migration from Zimbabwe. The key ones are the economic decline in the 2000s and a political environment that became repressive. Irregular migration and what some term 'survival migration' by the poor, as well as cross-border trade, was one of the forms that circular migration took as the economic crisis pushed out migrants in search of basic livelihoods. The chapter then examines the scale of remittance flows back into the country. A distinction is made between formal and informal forms of remittance that makes it difficult to estimate the scale of flows. Masiiwa and Chilunjika are upbeat about the potential of Diaspora remittances and skills to contribute to Zimbabwe's development. They make pertinent policy recommendations for how migration can deepen investment, remittances and trade flows.

A project of this scope should put at its centre those social forces that are often marginalised. Key questions relate to the forms and consequences of demographic change. The population has multiplied in a few decades. The youth now constitute the majority of the population, yet they have little power, influence or resources.

Under this thematic area, there is an exploration of the challenges that the youth experience, including unemployment, limited skills opportunities and political marginalisation (Hodzi 2014; Chimwara 2019). How can the youth be meaningfully integrated into the development and governance processes? Gender discrimination continues to plague the Zimbabwean society. This results in the comparative marginalisation of women in social, economic and political life.

The chapter by Rekopantswe Mate examines the link between the development process and social exclusion since independence with a particular focus on women and young people. Although both social groups are demographically dominant, they lack political, economic and cultural power to influence decisions. In the chapter, social exclusion is defined in relation to experiences of marginalised groups being left out of socio-economic and political institutions and processes through unemployment, underemployment, poverty and disenfranchisement. Marginalisation included being unable to earn an income or earning one erratically, being uneducated or unskilled and doing precarious informal work. Mate explores the social exclusion of women and youth by assessing four areas: work and employment, political participation and decision-making, education, and sexual and reproductive health.

Broadly speaking, structural barriers impede women and young people in systemic ways. The barriers include what Mate terms patriarchal cultural norms that are deeply ingrained in the Zimbabwean psyche. She observes that these norms with a gender bias pervade parliament, courts of law, traditional courts, the media and other institutions. Limited participation and decision-making by women ensures their low visibility in the corridors of power (RAU, 2015).

Similarly, young people are politically under-represented. The chapter observes that there are no political protocols, quotas and affirmative action programmes to ensure meaningful youth participation and development. A possible outcome was that, as excluded as they are, young people increasingly resorted to 'rhizomatic politics', power and resistance, and political action that spread below the radar of those in power. Mate concludes with specific recommendations to promote the social inclusion of these groups in development and representation. A Conclusion, that also explores the socio-economic impact of COVID-19, forms the last part of the book.

References

Arrighi, G. (1973) 'Labour Supplies in Historical Perspective: A Study of the Proletarianisation of the African Peasantry in Rhodesia', in G. Arrighi and J. Saul (eds) *Essays on the Political Economy of Africa*. New York: Monthly Review Press.

Alexander, J., J. McGregor and T. Ranger (2000) *Violence and Memory: One Hundred years in the 'Dark Forests' of Matabeleland*. Oxford: James Currey; Harare: Weaver Press.

Auditor General (2019) *2019 Report of the Auditor General*. Harare: Government Printer.

Banana, C. (1989) *Turmoil and Tenacity*. Harare: College Press.

Bratton, M. (2014) *Power Politics in Zimbabwe*. Boulder, CO: Lynne Rienner.

———— and E. Masunungure (2011) 'The Anatomy of Political Predation: Leaders, Elites and Coalitions in Zimbabwe, 1980-2010'. Development Leadership Program, Research Paper 09.

Catholic Commission for Justice and Peace in Zimbabwe (CCJPZ) and Legal Resources Foundation (1997) *Breaking the Silence, Building true Peace: A Report on the Disturbances in Matabeleland and the Midlands, 1980 to 1988*. Harare: CCJPZ and LRF.

Chimwara, O. (2019) 'Youth Participation in the Democratic Process in the Zimbabwean Elections'. Mimeo.

Chipika, J.T. and J.A. Malaba (2017) 'Towards a Transformative Democratic Developmental State in Zimbabwe – the Complex Journey', in Kanyenze et al. 2017.

Cliffe, L. and C. Stoneman (1989) *Zimbabwe: Politics, Economics and Society*. London: Pinter.

Edigheji, O. (ed.) (2010) *Constructing a democratic developmental state in South Africa*. Cape Town: HSRC Press.

European Union Election Observer Mission (EU EOM) (2018) *Final Report of Republic of Zimbabwe Harmonised Elections*. Brussels: EU.

Frank, A.G. (1967) *Capitalism and Underdevelopment in Latin America: Historical Studies of Chile and Brazil*. New York: Monthly Review Press.

Government of Zimbabwe (GoZ) (1991) 'Framework for Economic Reform 1991-95'. Harare: Government Printer.

———— (2013) Zimbabwe Agenda for Programme for Sustainable Socio-Economic Transformation (ZimAsset). Harare: Government Printer.

———— (2018) *Transitional Stabilisation Programme*. Harare: Government Printer.

———— (2018) *Towards an Upper-Middle Income Economy by 2030*. Harare: Government Printer.

Gibbon, P. (ed.) (1995) *Structural Adjustment and the Working Poor in Zimbabwe*. Uppsala: Nordic Africa Institute.

Hammar, A., B. Raftopoulos and S. Jensen (eds) (2003) *Zimbabwe's Unfinished Business: Rethinking Land, State and Nation in the Context of Crisis*. Harare: Weaver Press.

Hodzi, O. (2014) 'The Youth Factor in Zimbabwe's Harmonised Elections', *Journal of African Elections*, 13(2), pp. 48-70.

———— (2018) 'Economic Crisis, Structural Change and the Devaluation of Labour', in L. Sachikonye, B. Raftopoulos and G. Kanyenze (eds), *Building from the Rubble: The Labour Movement in Zimbabwe since 2000*. Harare: Weaver Press.

————, T. Kondo, P. Chitambara and J. Martens (eds) (2011) *Beyond the Enclave: Towards a Pro-poor and Inclusive Development Strategy for Zimbabwe*. Harare: Weaver Press

————, H. Jauch, A.D. Kanengoni, M. Madzwamuse and D. Muchena (2017) *Towards Democratic Developmental States in Southern Africa*. Harare: Weaver Press

Kaulemu, D. (2004) 'The culture of party politics and the concept of the state', in D. Harold-Barry (ed.) *Zimbabwe: the Past is the Future*. Harare: Weaver Press.

———— (2019) 'National Dialogue: the Zimbabwean Experience and Prospects for the Future'. Mimeo.

Makochekanwa, A., E. Chitando, D. Motsi, N. Taruvinga and K. Mtero (2019) 'One Country, Different Worlds: inequality in Zimbabwe'. Mimeo.

Mandaza, I. (1986) *Zimbabwe: the Political Economy of Transition*. Dakar: Codesria.

———— and D. Peterson (eds) (2015) *Zimbabwe: The Challenges of Democratisation and Economic Recovery*. Harare: Sapes Books.

Masiiwa, M. (2019) 'Migration and Trade: optimizing economic benefits for Zimbabwe'. Mimeo.

Masiyiwa, S. (2016) *Breaking Through: How to build a multi-billion dollars business in Africa*. Published by Geophrey Tenganamba Keynes.

Masunungure, E. (2004) 'Travails of opposition politics in Zimbabwe since Independence', in D. Harold-Barry (ed.) Zimbabwe: *The Past is the Future*. Harare: Weaver Press.

Mkandawire, T. (2001) 'Thinking about developmental states in Africa', *Cambridge Journal of Economics*, 25(3), pp. 289-313

Motlanthe Commission (2018) *Report of the Commission of Inquiry into the 1st of August 2018 Post-Election Violence*. Harare: Government Printer.

Moyo, S., K. Helliker and T. Murisa (2008) *Contested Terrain: Land Reform and Civil Society in Contemporary Zimbabwe*. Pietermaritzburg: S & S Publishers.

Mukonori, F. (2012) *The Genesis of Violence in Zimbabwe*. Harare: Center for Peace Initiatives in Africa.

Murisa, T. and T. Chikweche (eds) (2016) *Beyond the Crises: Zimbabwe's Prospects for Transformation*. Harare: Trust Africa and Weaver Press.

PACT (2016) 'Beyond Strikes and Demonstrations: the future of citizen Activism in Zimbabwe'. Harare: PACT.

Raftopoulos, B. (ed.) (2013) *The Hard Road to Reform: The politics of Zimbabwe's Global Political Agreement*. Harare: Weaver Press.

―――― and L. Sachikonye (eds) (2001) *Striking Back: The Labour Movement and the Post-Colonial State in Zimbabwe 1980-2000*. Harare: Weaver Press.

Alexander, J., J. McGregor and T. Ranger (2000) *Violence and Memory: One Hundred Years in the 'Dark Forests' of Matabeleland*. Oxford: James Currey.

RAU (2015) *Seen but not heard: women's participation in Local Government in Zimbabwe*. Harare: RAU.

Reeler, T., (2017) 'Dealing with the Past: Considerations for transitional justice and setting up the National Peace and Reconciliation Commission'. Harare: RAU.

Rodney, W. (1972) *How Europe underdeveloped Africa*. London: Bogle-L'Ouverture Publications.

Sachikonye, L. (2012) *Zimbabwe's Lost Decade: Politics, Development and Society*. Harare: Weaver Press.

―――― (2017) 'The Protracted Democratic Transition in Zimbabwe', *Taiwan Journal of Democracy*, 13(1), pp. 117-136.

———— B. Raftopoulos and G. Kanyenze (eds) (2018) *Building from the Rubble: The Labour Movement in Zimbabwe since 2000.* Harare: Weaver Press.

Saunders, R. and T. Nyamunda (eds) (2016) *Facets of Power: Politics, Profits and People in the Making of Zimbabwe's Blood Diamonds.* Harare: Weaver Press.

Scoones, I., N. Marongwe, B. Mavedzenge, J. Mahenehene, F. Murimbarimba and C. Sukume (2010) *Zimbabwe's Land Reform, Myths & Realities.* Woodbridge: James Currey.

Sen, A. (1999) *Development as Freedom.* Oxford: Oxford University Press.

Shumba, J. M. (2018) *Zimbabwe's Predatory State: Party, Military and Business.* Pietermaritzburg: UKZN Press.

Simpson, M. and T. Hawkins (2018) *The Primacy of Regime Survival: State Fragility and Economic Destruction in Zimbabwe.* Cham: Palgrave Macmillan.

Steiner, A. and A. Dembowski (2020) 'Governance is fundamental', *Development and Cooperation*, September 2020.

Tengende, N. (1994) 'Workers, Students and Struggles for Democracy: State-Civil Society relations in Zimbabwe'. PhD thesis, Roskilde University.

———— (2001) 'Economic Liberalization and Public Sector Workers in Zimbabwe', in B. Beckman and L.M. Sachikonye (eds) *Labour Regimes and Liberalization: The Restructuring of State-Society Relations in Africa.* Harare: University of Zimbabwe Publications.

Transparency International Zimbabwe (TIZ) (2016) *2015 Annual State of Corruption: Political Economy of Corruption and the Battle for Accountability in Zimbabwe 2000-2015.* Harare: TIZ.

———— (2017) *Corruption and Cultural Dynamics in Zimbabwe.* Harare: TIZ.

———— (2018) *Let us break the corruption chain together.* Harare: TIZ

UNECA (2014) *Report on Symposium on the Developmental State.* Lusaka: UNECA.

UNDP (2008) *Comprehensive Economic Recovery in Zimbabwe: A Discussion Document.* Harare: UNDP.

———— (1998 to 2009) 'Human Development Reports'. New York: UNDP.

——— (2004) *Human Development Report 2004: Cultural Liberty in Today's Diverse World*. New York: UNDP.

Utete Report (2003) 'Report of the Presidential Land Review Committee on the Implementation of the Fast Track Land Reform Programme'. Harare: Government Printer.

World Bank (2019) 'Analysis of Spatial Patterns of Settlement, Internal Migration and Welfare Inequality in Zimbabwe'. Washington, DC: World Bank.

Zimbabwe Congress of Trade Unions (ZCTU) (1996) *Beyond ESAP*. Harare: ZCTU.

Zimbabwe Election Commission (ZEC) (2019) *Report on the 2018 Zimbabwe Election*. Harare: ZEC.

Zimbabwe Election Support Network (ZESN) (2018) *Report on the 2018 Zimbabwe Election*. Harare: ZESN.

ZHR NGO Forum (2019) *On the Days of Darkness in Zimbabwe*. Harare: ZHR NGO Forum.

2

Linking Values, Institutions and Development in Zimbabwe

David Kaulemu

Introduction

Culture and values inform and are, in turn, informed by how society is ordered in terms of its structures, systems and institutions (Poole 1991: ix). Cultural values are about how societies identify, promote and respect what is good, admirable or praiseworthy and discourage and condemn what is bad, cruel and unjust. What is identified as good or praiseworthy can be so in terms of moral and/or non-moral goodness, either of which can contribute to a good life (Frankena 1963: 48). A good life for an individual person, family, local community, country or nation is one that achieves a good life for its members, both in the moral and non-moral sense. As Frankena points out, a good life in the moral sense implies a social, political and economic life in which people, individually or in community, act according to virtue, justice and respect. A morally good life shuns corruption, violence, exploitation and oppression. A good life in the non-moral sense is one that is happy or satisfying in that people's needs and desires for material, social and spiritual goods are fulfilled. A good life in this non-moral sense is one in which human beings are educated, have a healthy long life, train for and find jobs that satisfy them, and have homes and opportunities for leisure and relaxation with their families.

Every society strives to cultivate virtues and morally good people for their own sake and yet also in the hope that happiness and fulfilment can be achieved. It is rare to find societies that publicly and deliberately encourage their citizens to search for their own happiness at the expense of virtue, justice and moral goodness. In this sense, development must be about the structures, processes and institutions of society that are designed to produce goods and services that fulfil peoples happiness as well as about 'what varieties of men and women now prevail in this society…?'(Mills 1992: 6) A well-ordered society (Rawls 1971: 453-462) is one that links its production patterns and economic institutions to fulfil human needs (Ekins, and Max-Neef 1992; Smith and Max-Neef 2011) and makes efforts to form people of virtue and integrity whose manner of production and consumption are directed towards care and the common good and do not threaten social peace and the environment.

Values, both moral and non-moral, inspire members of society to build social systems in certain ways and yet those very systems also help to form their values. Values guide how people measure the worthiness of their lives and the natural and social environments around them. Values inform approaches to national development and shape the form and content of that development. Development itself is a value. People and organisations work to achieve it. For example, the UNDP, which in many ways represents the global aspirations of nations, defines development as being 'about allowing people to lead the kind of life they choose and providing them with the tools and opportunities to make those choices' (UNDP 2004: v). It is also about enlarging human capacity and capability, longevity and happiness (UNDP 1990: 1-7). Amartya Sen, who has influenced the spirit of the UNDP reports, sees development as a process of expanding the realm that people enjoy: substantive freedoms that include avoiding deprivations such as starvation, undernourishment, escapable morbidity and premature mortality as well as freedoms associated with being literate and numerate, and enjoying political participation and uncensored speech (Sen 1999: 36).

This chapter follows the UNDP approach to development, and explores the relationships and dynamics between culture, traditions, values and institutional structures that either facilitate or impede the development process and how they shape and inform it. It tracks, in broad terms, the values influencing visions and practices of development in Zimbabwe since before independence. It unpacks underlying ideological values that motivate dominant development efforts and institutions, and inspire different sections of the society in struggles for survival, human flourishing and environmental justice. The chapter rejects 'claims that cultural differences necessarily lead to social, economic and political conflict' (UNDP 2004: v). It assesses the success and failure of the values and principles informing existing policy development directions at this stage of the country's history and argues that we now have enough evidence to demonstrate that certain ways of conducting ourselves as a nation and as leaders have failed. It locates the root cause of national developmental impasse in the failure by sections of the Zimbabwean population and their leaders to go beyond pre-independence exclusivist narratives in order to cultivate truly inclusive national solidarity. It points to the development of new national narratives that could be key to unlocking Zimbabwe's developmental impasse.

Values, politics and institutions

Values explain why we join certain political parties, social movements and religious traditions and not others. They explain why we are in favour of building and strengthening certain institutions rather than others. Values therefore inform our politics, our morality and how we think our personal, local, national and global development should proceed. Values are expressed more by what we do than by what we say. We sometimes say we believe that women are equal to men, yet the history and politics of our political and economic institutions demonstrate the opposite (see Mate in this volume). Most people, especially politicians, say they value peace and yet social and political violence is prevalent in the country. Key questions that could test our practical values and the morality of our politics include the following: When will Zimbabwe be led by a woman president who is not an ex-combatant? Do the majority of our citizens believe that Joshua Nkomo was as much a Zimbabwean as Robert Mugabe? When we say we are a democracy, why should the leadership of the country only be reserved for ZANU-PF men with the support of security forces, guns and tear gas? Why are third generation citizens of this country still being referred to as aliens? Why is Judith Garfield Todd not officially recognised as a Zimbabwean when her father was the prime minister of the country? (Todd 2012: 39-49). This looks like the same madness as Fredrick Chiluba's attempt to declare Kenneth Kaunda, the first president of Zambia, a foreigner. These questions point to some of the major fault lines that have not been adequately attended to and are major obstacles to Zimbabwe's inclusive national growth and development. These fault lines explain the social disasters that have stood in the way of development, including the failure to make the appropriate distinctions between the ruling party, government and the state (Kaulemu 2004: 79), *Gukurahundi* (CCJPZ and LRF 1997), *Murambatsvina* (Tibaijuka 2005), the poorly planned Fast Track Land Reform Programme, party-politicised national institutions and post-election violence. All these processes expose our hypocrisy as we publicly claim to value national unity, peace and social justice while we, in practice, sow the seeds of divisions, suspicions, violence and injustice. A mature society is one that cultivates humility and tracks its own hypocrisy by 'accepting boldly the gap between principles and practice, between promise and performance' (West 1993: 5) and then goes on to make efforts to close the gap.

One of the best ways in which we defend our values is to ritualise and institutionalise them. We develop rituals and traditions around the events, people and symbols that stand for our values. We also build organisations, institutions, and social structures that promote these values and symbols we say we value. For example, we say we value independence. This is why we fought for the establishment of the Zimbabwe nation state. The national investment into the constitution making process demonstrates the level of our commitment to the rule of law. The level of our commitment to peace is seen in the establishment of the Lancaster House Agreement in 1979, the National Unity Accord in 1987, the Unity Government in 2013 (Chigora and Guzura 2011) and the National Peace and Reconciliation Commission. The list of national symbols, monuments, commemorations and holidays suggests what the nation regards as of national value. The fact that we celebrate the fortieth year of independence shows how we value freedom and independence, even though we may have different views about them. This chapter explains why these major national values and principles have not been realised. It has to do with the kinds of stories that Zimbabweans tell about themselves and about each other, and with what Taylor (1994) calls 'the politics of recognition' and the politics of identity and citizenship.

Contextualising values in Zimbabwe at 40

Zimbabweans have multi-ethnic, multi-cultural, multi-racial origins. Hence there are fundamental differences in what kind of stories they tell. These differences do not have to lead to violent conflicts that undermine development, yet in Zimbabwe, they do. This explains why we may establish institutions for peace, for example, and yet not give them the resources for them to succeed. It may explain why local government councils which have been controlled by opposition political parties since 2000, have not received requisite support from central government structures that are controlled by ZANU-PF. It explains why certain regions of the country have been neglected and why some Zimbabweans have lost their citizenship and their children struggle to get birth certificates. It explains why we may not have a woman president for a very long time and why we struggle to see white Africans as Zimbabweans and why white Zimbabweans struggle to see themselves as Africans.

A dramatic taste of these deep divisions was experienced when the Zimbabwe Catholic Bishops' Conference published a pastoral letter entitled 'The March is not Ended'. They were talking about the 'march for freedom'. Quoting the late American civil rights leader, John Robert Lewis, they described this fundamental national disagreement over the meaning and value of freedom in the following words:

> The march for freedom is not ended even in the present time in which we live. This too is our challenge in Zimbabwe today between those who believe in a past and completed liberation and those who realize that the march is not ended. Peace building and nation-building are never completed tasks. Every generation has to establish national cohesion and peace (ZCBC 2020).

Some sections of the population feel that they have the appropriate values for the development of the country. Others think this is not the case. The ZANU-PF government appears to take the former view which suggests that Zimbabwe as a nation has come to 'the end of history' (Fukuyama, 1992) in the sense that, after political liberation in 1980, we can learn no new insights about freedom and no one can teach the liberation movement anything more about democracy. Francis Fukuyama's idea of 'the end of history' has proved problematic. Zimbabweans need time to allow the constituents of the country to engage each other to facilitate understanding and development. As Anthony Giddens (1991: 54) and Charles Taylor (1984) have emphasised, 'In order to have a sense of who we are, we have to have a notion of how we have become, and of where we are going'.

Historians have engaged this question by asking what different sections of the population think about who they are, how they have become and where they are going in relation to Zimbabwe. The values we need as a nation, must be able to take each section of the population beyond its own 'common sense' (Bauman 1992: 7) its 'naïve consciousness' (Freire 2000: 61) and its comfort zone in order to expand its imagined sense of community to embrace other communities that have invested their lives and resources in the country. This demands widening the moral world of each community and deepening its moral sense. To the extent that the post-colonial leadership of the country has attempted to restrict the national ethical landscape to the 'inner core of the Shona historical experience' (Mudenge 1988: 364), they may have failed to provide a wide enough moral foundation for the country's future development.

Zimbabwe, because of its history, means different things to different people. This is both a major challenge and an opportunity for how the country is to develop. It is a challenge when each community, each class, each political movement, insists on staying in its cultural and ethical comfort zone and tries to universalise its own particularity. It is an opportunity when communities recognise the beauty of 'letting a hundred flowers bloom', and are keen to learn from others by innovating and experimenting with new relationships and new ethical demands. As Giddens (1992:14) writes, this kind of experience is the '*reflexivity* of modernity'. Zimbabwe is in a situation that requires 'morality without ethics' (**Bauman** 1995: 10) and engagement without preconditions.

Current ways of imagining Zimbabwe shield us from seeing opportunities for growth and development. For example, the national wealth we have lost through *Gukurahundi*, *Murambatsvina* and the violence of the Fast Track Land Reform Progrmme are unrecoverable. Raftopoulos and Mlambo (2009), explain the root cause of this problem. Contestation around these issues of national identity, citizenship, who belongs, sovereignty and who has what rights explain a lot about why Zimbabwe is where it is today. With a self-confident political leadership imbued with epistemological humility, and a progressive cosmopolitan common social imaginary, Zimbabweans could construct more inclusive narratives that can facilitate greater prospects for human and environmental flourishing. A self-confident political leadership is not afraid of democracy and neither does it try to suppress fundamental human freedoms. It tries to contribute to building a society that respects and encourages basic human rights. Such leadership accepts its own weaknesses and is prepared to allow others to take their turn in legitimate national governance. No individual or group of individuals has a monopoly over leadership knowledge and skills.

Debates on the ontological and ethical status of Zimbabwe

Dominant ways of imagining Zimbabwe have been so narrow that they have alienated many, and have prevented significant numbers of people from participating fully in the country's economics, politics and culture. This has prevented the country from mobilising enough social capital to support its desired economic development. Bhandari and Yasunobu (2009) explain that this capital is made up of relationships in form of social networks, civic engagements, norms of reciprocity and general trust that 'facilitates cooperation and collective action for mutual benefit'.

Mahmood Mamdani (1996) has helped us to understand how colonial systems constructed the legacies of 'citizens' and 'subjects' in African societies. Historians describe how colonial and post-colonial political authorities encouraged the development of narrow and exclusivist historical accounts of the country. Kaulemu (2011: 104) notes that, 'Since 1890, Zimbabwe as a nation-state has always been monopolised by a few.' Each group, supported by sympathetic historians, artists, writers and other analysts, gives its own interpretation of history and sociology which downplays, ignores or demonises the role of others while legitimising its own. Different shades of settler regimes spread their views through colonial laws, and various versions of democracy, education, culture, sport, and religion; the nature of their national and local government budgets reflected their values (De La Torre 2004). Clear examples of the influence of colonial values on development priorities are Rhodesia's Land Apportionment Act of 1930 and the colonial education policies (Richards and Govere 2003). At political independence the ontological status of the country was widened to include more people and traditions, especially black people, but it continued and still continues to leave out many people. This failure to recognise sections of society and their contributions, for whatever reason, is a major problem for Zimbabwe in its desire to develop. This means Zimbabwe is unable to tap into the intellectual, spiritual, cultural, economic and political resources of its own citizens. Divisions of all forms, inequalities and exclusions have been too expensive for Zimbabwe to be developmentally viable (Lansley 2012). As Mlambo observes,

> ....there was, thus, little in the ethnic, racial and cultural past of Zimbabwe before, during and after colonialism that had laid an adequate and appropriate foundation for the development of a

common national identity or an efficient modern state with a commitment to the welfare of its entire people. Colonial rule and the anticolonial armed struggle that it provoked had polarised the population along mainly racial lines, while struggle movements were divided along largely ethnic lines, in what Zimbabwean political scientist Masipula Sithole (1979) has characterised as 'struggles within the struggle'. Meanwhile, postcolonial government policies and practices did little to unify the country (Mlambo 2013: 54).

The challenge facing Zimbabwe today is, first and foremost, a spiritual challenge. 'Spiritual' here refers to the major inspirational motivations that make sense of the ontology of an imagined community as it reflexively constructs and reconstructs itself (Giddens 1991:72). Spirituality emanates from what is assumed to be there as an existence, i.e. 'what there is' (Quine 1980). An understanding of 'what there is' suggests emotional attachment and response. The attempt to separate facts from values, based on David Hume's 'fork' (Snare 1992: 76), the 'is/ought' distinction, is a sham (Skillen 1977). Moral prescriptions and obligations are implicated and suggested in the descriptions of what there is. Zygmunt Bauman (1992) insisted that a social analyst, as opposed to a physicist, is always implicated in the social phenomena he or she analyses. This is why millions of people have died for what they consider to be their nations (O'Hear 1985).

The fact of parenthood, friendship or citizenship, implies moral obligations on the part of parents, friends and the state. The fact of nationhood also implies emotional attachments and moral obligations (Poole 1991: 90-109). This point does not preclude the claim that Anderson makes that nationalism is an artefact (ibid.: 107); it means that the way the facts of nationhood are described implicate what emotional responses will ensue. Certain ways of characterising the nation alienate and exclude some communities and their contributions. Zimbabwe needs to find ways of presenting itself as a nation that will invite all to participate and contribute to it. The national narratives and the implicated emotional attachments and moral obligations are the foundations of whatever else the nation will be capable of achieving socially, politically and economically. No national institution can escape the implications of this fact. Unfortunately for Zimbabwe, the social divisions and political hostilities have paralysed and poisoned many national processes and made many of its institutions dysfunctional. For example, such institutions as the courts, the security forces, the Zimbabwe Electoral Commission, the National Peace and Reconciliation Commission and the National Prosecution Authority are not trusted by many citizens as truly national institutions (Feltoe 2004).

Sorting out national priorities

Many analysts believe that Zimbabwe's main challenges are economic and political, including President Mnangagwa's government, which has called for the prioritisation of economic strategies. Yet the major national challenges have remained unsolved. Mawowa and McCandless (2018) suggest that, 'Political settlements in Zimbabwe have been elite-driven and failed to address core conflict issues'. They argue that agreements such as the Lancaster House Settlement, the Unity Accord, the Global Political Agreement, and the November 2017 'New Dispensation' failed to meet the necessary conditions required of any resilient social contract:

- * Political settlements and social contract-making mechanisms must be inclusive and responsive to 'core conflict issues'.
- * Institutions (formal, customary, and informal) need to be increasingly effective and inclusive and to have broadly shared outcomes that meet societal expectations and enhance state legitimacy.
- * Social cohesion must broaden and deepen, with formal and informal ties and interactions binding society horizontally (across citizens, between groups) and vertically (between citizens/groups and the state) (ibid.).

Social contract conditions – unless they address the social imaginaries informing the self-understanding of participants and their recognition and non-recognition in the social contracts – are too thin to be successful. The social and moral order assumed by the participants of the political settlements will determine whether the social contract-making mechanisms are inclusive. In fact, the question of who is included or recognised and who is not, is the 'core conflict issue'. Political settlements and social-contract mechanisms in Zimbabwe will not be inclusive as long as 'the discourse to simplify issues of identity and recognition' (Taylor 1994) are not addressed.

Modern institutions require equality in the treatment of citizens. Citizens in modern legal institutions of countries like Zimbabwe are understood in their individual capacities. But how can we insist on treating citizens in this individualised sense when citizens have come from different historical and cultural backgrounds, including from backgrounds that respect hierarchies and social embeddedness? What does it mean for modern 'Public institutions, including government agencies, schools, and liberal arts colleges and universities' to recognise or respect the particular cultural identities of citizens? (ibid.: 34) This question has not been settled for Zimbabwe and no formal platforms have been created to get citizens to negotiate appropriate responses to it. Explaining the process of identity formation and social recognition, Taylor (ibid.) argues that:

> … my discovering my own identity doesn't mean that I work it out in isolation, but that I negotiate it through dialogue, partly overt, partly internal, with others. …My own identity crucially depends on my dialogical relations with others.

The development of identity and social recognition described here applies not just to individuals but also to groups and cultures. Zimbabwe has not created the space or time to facilitate this development of a Zimbabwean identity that facilitates self-recognition and recognition by others that is respectful and consistent with values of democracy and human rights. For as long as we continue to avoid this dialogical engagement, it is difficult to see how our public institutions can be inclusive, and social cohesion be widened and deepened.

The perils of imagining citizenship in Zimbabwe

In 2012, The African Forum for Catholic Social Teaching (AFCAST), in association with the Konrad Adenauer Stiftung, ran a book project on how Zimbabweans imagined nationhood and citizenship. Articles were solicited 'to bring out how that imagination (of nationhood and citizenship) has influenced political, economic, social and cultural developments in Zimbabwe' (Kaulemu 2012: v). Here is what the editor of the book wrote in his introduction,

> The responses to this call were telling. My own reading of the responses could itself be telling. There was a general reluctance to talk explicitly about the ontological and spiritual identity of Zimbabwe and how that identity informs the ways in which citizenship is imagined. There are many questions that Zimbabweans still hesitate to talk about in public, even though we will sometimes admit to our prejudices in private. As Zimbabweans, we shy away from public discourse unless we are assured of acceptance and victory. The universal common good

is alien to our psyche. Since 1890, we have never really accepted multiculturalism. In many ways we are colonial subjects who have imbibed colonialist exclusivism with a vengeance.

In the same anthology, Diana Jeater demonstrates how deep this question of the social imaginary is when she interrogates why ZANU-PF continues to hold power and electoral support even though it is violent, incompetent and authoritarian. She tries 'to understand the un-coerced affinity with ZANU-PF that is still felt in many rural areas, which seems rooted in something more visceral, or perhaps more spiritual, than political affiliation alone.'(Jeater 2012: 124) She writes:

> Neither partisan, oppressive behaviour by the state nor unprecedented economic collapse significantly undermined rural people's willingness to vote for the primary perpetrators of the political violence, ZANU-PF. The MDC, meanwhile, found that its platform of defending citizenship, civil society and property rights seemed too often to fall on stony ground. Why has the MDC not been able to build up a stronger sense in Zimbabwe of the citizen and a citizen's rights vis-à-vis the state?

Analysts argue that the country needs effective and inclusive institutions as well as social cohesion modelled on a social contract. Jeater raises the question of whether enough has been done to interrogate the moral and spiritual foundation and the social imaginary behind ZANU-PF support. She points to the fact that while a lot of effort has been put into building democratic institutions and procedures, the spiritual and moral order informing most citizens' sense of self is still not consistent with those institutions. For example, in spite of what the Constitution says, many ordinary Zimbabweans think in term of the categories of Shona versus Ndebele and indigenous versus foreigner, where 'foreigner' may include people whose parents were born in Zimbabwe and who have never lived anywhere else. So, citizens can go through elections without necessarily committing to the modern imaginary appropriate to the process. In public, political leaders present themselves as committed to human rights, the rule of law and democratic processes and yet they still conjure up feudalistic images of being 'fathers' and 'mothers' of the nation. They still treat citizens as if they were children who need to be told how to vote. This is demonstrated in post-election violence in which citizens are punished by the ruling party and government forces for voting for opposition parties (Sachikonye 2011: 49). Opposition political parties are legally registered according to the Zimbabwean law and yet their members are treated by the law as if they were foreign hostile forces.

Broadly speaking, the social, political and economic challenges the country faces are really symptoms of a deeper spiritual and moral crisis that stems from lack of 'the adequate and appropriate foundation' that Mlambo talks about. The country has neglected to build the spirit that informs:

> ... the ways people imagine their social existence, how they fit together with others, how things go on between them and their fellows, the expectations that are normally met, and the deeper normative notions and images that underlie these expectations (Taylor 2004: 23).

For national politics, culture and economics to be sustainable, the country and indeed the whole world needs this morality and spirituality to become the cement of the national and global universe.

The Zimbabwe we want

To be fair, there have been efforts to engage the identity question and the politics of recognition. In 2006, in the spirit of Christian values, the Zimbabwe Catholic Bishops' Conference, the Evangelical Fellowship of Zimbabwe, and the Zimbabwe Council of Churches came together as the Heads of Christian Denominations to invite the nation to a national visioning process, and produced a National Vision Document entitled *The Zimbabwe We Want*. They invited the nation to reflect on this document with a view to making their contributions. They also invited the government to engage with the process, but unfortunately it was manipulated by the Mugabe government, politicised by some actors and ignored by most Zimbabweans. In addition, the document itself, and the processes it initiated, did not deal with fundamental identity and recognition questions. This became a lost opportunity and a practical demonstration of how the toxic polarised national spirituality renders all efforts for national development dysfunctional.

The legacy of weak and conflicting spiritual and ethical foundations

Recognition of the complexity of Zimbabwe as a social and political formation is critical in determining its ontological status and developing the moral vision that informs its development. This ontological and subsequent ethical need is being acknowledged by a significant number of historians and other professionals. For instance, Ndlovu-Gatsheni (2009: 46) explains the ontological and ethical complexities that call for a multi-faceted and multi-layered appreciation of Zimbabwe:

> ... like all historically and socially constructed phenomena, [Zimbabwe] is exceedingly difficult to define. It is a complex mosaic of contending histories and memories, making it as much a reality as it is an idea, a construction not only moulded out of precolonial, colonial and nationalist pasts, but also out of global values of sovereignty, self-determination and territorial integrity. It is an idea born out of continuing synthesis of multilayered, overlapping and cross-pollinating historical genealogies, and contending nationalisms, as well as suppressed local and regional sovereignties.

The challenge of development for Zimbabwe has been the failure, and sometimes the refusal, to recognise and appreciate the ethical implications of this complex history. Instead, there has been an attempt to narrow and simplify it by banishing all ambiguous and ambivalent legacies. Hence the development of narrow exclusivist moral visions which have made it difficult to construct and cultivate the all-inclusive political visibility and social solidarity that could inspire and be the basis of the desired national development. After independence, the hope was for this inclusive recognition and solidarity to be established and institutionalised in order to harness all possible contributions. But 40 years later, we are still divided and reluctant to positively acknowledge each other's national contributions. This has been tragic as we have seen, over the last 130 years, the use of national institutions to neglect, restrict and destroy national treasures simply because they have been identified as belonging to groups not recognised by those in power.

How we got here

The national post-colonial political leaders attempted to monopolise power by giving and using a narrow historical account of Zimbabwe. At independence, superficial efforts were made to create an inclusive government that included members of parties other than ZANU-PF. It was not long before these efforts were shattered and the circle of those regarded as true members of the nation retrogressively narrowed. Mlambo (2013: 54) demonstrates that this amounts to:

> a self-serving oversimplification of the country's past meant to legitimise ZANU-PF rule as the logical and rightful successor to Zimbabwe's precolonial rulers of what was then, ostensibly, a united Shona nation. The reality is very different.

Stan Mudenge (1988: 364), a Zimbabwean historian and a prominent member of Mugabe's leadership, stressed this narrow account, when he concluded that:

> Present Zimbabwe, therefore, is not merely a 'geographical expression' created by imperialism during the nineteenth century. It is a reality that has existed for centuries, with a language, a culture and a 'worldview' of its own, representing the inner core of the Shona historical experience … present Zimbabweans have, both materially and culturally, much to build and not a little to build upon.

Mugabe insisted on this account of 'the inner core of the Shona historical experience', which assumed Zimbabwe to be a 'natural "Shona" nation' (Mlambo 2013: 54). Terence Ranger called this 'patriotic history' (Raftopoulos and Mlambo 2009: 53), which Mugabe tried to teach in schools and promote in national newspapers and other mass media. National policies reflected this narrow historical perspective. The spirituality behind 'patriotic history' can be used to understand major developments in the struggles for independence and the post-colonial policies of Mugabe's leadership. It can explain the historical tensions between ZANU-PF and PF ZAPU and how these culminated in *Gukurahundi* and the sustained developmental neglect of the Matabeleland regions (Hadebe 2015).

Mazarire (2009) demonstrates the complexity of Zimbabwe's pre-colonial history. He shows that the history is made up of the stories of the large states and empires that rose and fell, but also of the 'small societies' that had links to their 'parent' societies. Using Mazarire's analysis, Mlambo (2013: 54) rightly concludes that:

> The lived experiences of the people now known as Zimbabweans do not sustain patriotic history's claim that Zimbabwe has always been a nation. In fact, Zimbabwe has always been a land of

different communities with different cultures and histories whose collective lives cannot be recounted through one single historical narrative.

One way in which the lived experiences of Zimbabweans contradict patriotic history is demonstrated by 'struggles within the struggle'. The epistemological widening of Zimbabwean historiography has contributed to the widening of the national imagination. Yet this is still not enough. Munochiveyi (2011) argues for more work to be done to widen the range of sites of struggle and the voices of those who have been marginalised by patriotic and nationalist histories. ZANU-PF has been resilient in defending patriotic history and reinventing itself and its arguments often supported by teargas, arrests, abductions, police raids and military operations (Sachikonye 2011).

Widening the mind and deepening ethical responses

Human beings now live in situations that challenge both our knowledge, social imaginations and emotional responses. Wright Mills (2000) summarises the modern predicament:

> The very shaping of history now outpaces the ability of men to orient themselves in accordance with cherished values. And which values? Even when they do not panic, men often sense that older ways of feeling and thinking have collapsed and that newer beginnings are ambiguous to the point of moral stasis. Is it any wonder that ordinary men feel they cannot cope with the larger worlds with which they are so suddenly confronted?

This predicament is being faced by all human beings on earth as we struggle to make sense of the COVID-19 pandemic and new movements such as Black Lives Matter. Mills argues that these challenges require the development of 'a quality of mind' that he calls 'the sociological imagination'. However, he recognises that the sociological imagination 'is found in the social and psychological sciences, but it goes far beyond these studies as we now know them' and it 'enables us to grasp history and biography and the relations between the two within society' (ibid). Jeffrey Sachs (2008: 3) expresses the same point but emphasises the difficulties of grasping the links between biography and history:

> The defining challenge of the twenty-first century will be to face the

reality that humanity shares a common fate on a crowded planet. That common fate will require new forms of global cooperation, a fundamental point of blinding simplicity that many world leaders have yet to understand or embrace. For the past two hundred years, technology and demography have consistently run ahead of deeper social understanding. Industrialization and science have created a pace of change unprecedented in human history. Philosophers, politicians, artists, and economists must scramble constantly to catch up with contemporaneous social conditions. Our social philosophies, as a result, consistently lag behind present realities.

What is critical here is the recognition that a certain 'quality of mind' is demanded by contemporary circumstances. This 'quality of mind' is both about grappling with information and about searching for appropriate ethical responses to the human condition. This search is based on the assumption that while old ethical values are important, they may be found wanting even though we cannot begin our search without them. Bauman (1992) describes this in terms of moving from 'common sense' to 'thinking sociologically'. Paulo Freire (2013) describes it in terms of moving from 'naïve consciousness' to 'critical consciousness'. For Bauman (1992), while common sense is indispensable as a starting point for knowledge, it needs to be widened and deepened. He concludes:

> One could say that the main service the art of thinking sociologically may render to each and every one of us is to make us more sensitive; it may sharpen up our senses, open our eyes wider so that we can explore human conditions, which thus far had remained invisible.
> ….
> To think sociologically means to understand a little more fully the people around us, their cravings and dreams, their worries and their misery. We may then better appreciate the human individuals in them and perhaps even have more respect for their rights to do what we ourselves are doing and to cherish doing it. … Eventually, sociological thinking may well promote solidarity between us. A solidarity grounded in mutual understanding and respect, solidarity in our joint resistance to suffering and shared condemnation of the cruelty that causes it.

While Mills and Bauman talk of the quality of mind in terms of 'sociological imagination' and 'thinking sociologically', they are very clear that it goes beyond sociology. They point out that this quality of mind can be found in the best literature, journalism, psychology and philosophy, and can be promoted through art, poetry and music. I read Mlambo as promoting this quality of mind through a certain way of studying and teaching history. In his inaugural lecture on the occasion of becoming the new head of the Department of Historical and Heritage Studies at the University of Pretoria on 30 October 2012 Mlambo made the following statement:

> Clearly, historians and historiography are important in shaping society's self-perception, particularly societies such as our own that are struggling to develop common national identities and to establish states that are truly inclusive, in the wake of rather traumatic, divisive and acrimonious pasts in which one dominant group presided over a system that marginalised the majority and effectively wrote them out of history. The danger today, as is becoming evident in Zimbabwe, is that with the ascendancy of the African majority to political power throughout Southern Africa there may simply be an inversion of the previous dispensation, in which history is now used to marginalise the former dominant white groups, who in turn may well be written out of national histories.

Mlambo then goes on to call on history teachers to cultivate students with a quality of mind that helps them 'to produce historical accounts that are as unbiased as possible so as to provide a context in which members of past antagonistic groups can understand each other better and, hopefully, find each other'.

Defining the social imaginary

If – and it is a big if – Zimbabwe is to be built into a viable nation-state, it must develop the appropriate intellectual understanding and emotional attachments appropriate to this kind of project. Cumulative historical, sociological and anthropological evidence demonstrates that 'Zimbabwe like most African states created by colonialism, is not yet a nation and it is only in the process of becoming one' (Mlambo 2013). Ndlovu-Gatsheni (2011) illustrates that the attempt by the ZANU-PF post-colonial party and government to develop, and 'maintain a hegemonic and monologic narrative of the nation' has failed. Like many other analysts, he reminds us of the many 'struggles within the struggle' (Sithole 1979) and 'the struggles after the struggle' (Kaulemu 2008) that demonstrate the lack of a common social imaginary that could act as the foundation of Zimbabwean nation-building and state-formation.

Imaginaries are important because they inform how members of society treat each other and how they respond to each other. They inform their friendships, enmities and modes of governance. If they imagine their nation to be like a small village with chiefs and headman, that imagination will inform how they conduct their business and how they treat each other. If they imagine their society as characterised by divisions, hostility and war, this imagination will shape their attitudes and emotional responses to issues of governance.

Taylor makes an important distinction between social imaginary and social theory. For him, social theory is what academics and intellectual theories invent to understand social reality. As such, social theories are based on models and language that individual analysts develop in order to make sense of social reality. They are therefore shared by small groups of people, usually historians, sociologists and philosophers. Social imaginaries on the other hand are 'the way ordinary people "imagine" their social surroundings' (Taylor 2004: 23). Social imaginaries are therefore 'shared by large groups of people, if not the whole society' and are 'that common understanding that makes possible common practices and a widely shared sense of legitimacy' (ibid). Taylor argues that the lack of a shared social imaginary that is consistent with democratic practice and informs our social engagements is at the centre of Zimbabwe's multiple crises. This social imaginary can be built if we cultivate a certain understanding and ethical practice of civil society.

The ideal of civil society and movement to democracy and development

The idea of civil society has a long history and means different things to different people. I take, from its complex history, the suggestion that it is a realm that makes a 'synthesis of private and public "good" and of individual and social desiderata' (Seligman 1992: x). As Seligman points out, the idea 'embodies for many an ethical ideal of the social order'. It is a realm that recognises, respects and facilitates the growth and fulfilment of individuals, groups, and associations. It does not seek to annihilate those individuals, groups, communities and solidarities that do not conform to some a priori arbitrary standard. It is this idea of civil society that could act as a paradigm for the fight for equality and for democratic politics in Zimbabwe, in Africa and the world in general.

The good news is that there are signs that this ethical ideal is being realised in some areas of national, regional and world politics. There is greater respect for the different characters and cultural backgrounds of people in international forums. As the UNDP (2004) pointed out:

> Cultural liberty is a vital part of human development because being able to choose one's identity – who one is – without losing the respect of others or being excluded from other choices is important in leading a full life. People want the freedom to practice their religion openly, to speak their language, to celebrate their ethnic and religious heritage without fear of ridicule or punishment or diminished opportunity. People want the freedom to participate in society without having to slip off their chosen cultural moorings.

The undermining of civil society has been at the centre of many challenges of the modern world. Democracy is weakened when civil society is diminished (Putnam 2000). Modern society has seen the expansion of the state on the one hand, and the capitalist market on the other, at the expense of 'intermediate' institutions that can be the basis of a healthy society. These intermediate institutions are the family, and associations that are based on voluntary participation and solidarity. Although it is not entirely free of evils and injustices, civil society is the realm that builds the relationships that sustain society. In this sense any society wanting to pay attention to its social imaginaries in order to widen and deepen them for a multi-cultural, multi-racial and multi-religious society, will need to engage families and communities in order to help them engage each other. Civil society works with a unique logic. It contrasts itself to the logic of contracts found on the market and that of coercive public obligation of the state. Explaining this point, Pope Benedict (2009) writes:

> When both the logic of the market and the logic of the State come to an agreement that each will continue to exercise a monopoly over its respective area of influence,

in the long term much is lost: solidarity in relations between citizens, participation and adherence, actions of gratuitousness, all of which stand in contrast with giving in order to acquire (the logic of exchange) and giving through duty (the logic of public obligation, imposed by State Law)… The exclusive binary model of market-plus-State is corrosive of society, while economic forms based on solidarity, which find their natural home in civil society without being restricted to it, build up society. The market of gratuitousness does not exist, and attitudes of gratuitousness cannot be established by law. Yet both the market and politics need individuals who are open to reciprocal gift.

Thus for Pope Benedict, 'a strong civil sector is the basis of a healthy society and a healthy economy; economic contracts and state bureaucracies cannot hold a society together in peace, nor increase its solidarity' (ibid.). Civil society is the realm in which human beings meet as human beings and not as cogs in an economic or ideological political machine. This is critical in a society that needs to develop a new social imaginary out of dialogical engagements of people, families and communities emanating from different backgrounds and where conflicts and violence have characterised past engagements. For McLean (2005: 89) this helps,

… their efforts to become increasingly creative and to take responsibility for their life. This, in a way, is the utopian vision of Marx as people seek to realize the conditions of freedom to begin, with others, to shape their common life after the ideals of justice and peace, harmony and cooperation. As a result the focus of attention reaches beyond the political with its focus on power, and the economic with its focus on profit. It focuses upon its people, now no longer as amorphous masses or tools of industry, but as persons informed and responsible, uniting freely in human solidarities, to act responsibly and creatively each in their own field. This is the reality called civil society or civil culture emerging as a newly vibrant reality, which promises in contrast to the negative and skeptical critique of modernity to begin positively to shape a more globally sensitive 3rd millennium.

Conclusion

This realm of civil society is the new paradigm that can inform not only world politics and economics but also African social imaginaries and practices. African political leaders, especially those in Zimbabwe, need to rediscover this paradigm of civil society as it confirms their humanity, morality and agency. This rediscovery of human agency and enhanced human moral responsibility strikes a chord with the trends in Christian social teachings and in African traditional morality of Ubuntu. This is important for Zimbabwe as it creatively encourages the invention of new traditions for the future. All this must positively contribute to the development of Zimbabwe as it stands at a crossroads at the age of 40.

References

Bauman, Z. (1992) 'Thinking Sociologically', in A. Giddens, *Human Societies: An Introductory Reader in Sociology*. Cambridge: Polity Press.

——— (1995) *Life in Fragments: Essays in Postmodern Morality*. Oxford: Blackwell.

Bhandari, H. and K. Yasunobu (2009) 'What is Social Capital? A Comprehensive Review of the Concept', Asian Journal of Social Science, 37(3), pp. 480-510.

Catholic Commission for Justice and Peace in Zimbabwe (CCJPZ) and Legal Resources Foundation (1997) *Breaking the Silence, Building true Peace: A Report on the Disturbances in Matabeleland and the Midlands, 1980 to 1988*. Harare: CCJPZ and LRF.

Chigora, P. and T. Guzura (2011) 'The politics of the government of national unity (GNU) and power sharing in Zimbabwe: Challenges and prospects for democracy', *African Journal of History and Culture*, 3(2), pp. 20-26.

De La Torre, M.A. (2004) *Doing Christian Ethics from the Margins*. New York: Orbis Books.

Ekins, P. and M. Max-Neef (eds) (1992) *Real-Life Economics: Understanding Wealth Creation*. London: Routledge.

Feltoe, G. (2004) 'The onslaught against democracy and the rule of law in Zimbabwe in 2000,' in D. Harold-Barry (ed.) *Zimbabwe: the Past is the Future*. Harare: Weaver Press.

Frankena, W.K. (1963) *Ethics*. Englewood Cliffs, N.J.: Prentice-Hall.

Freire, P. (2000) 'Cultural Action for Freedom'. Harvard Educational Review: Monograph Series.

────── (2013) *Education for Critical Consciousness*. London: Bloomsbury.

Fukuyama, F. (1992) *The End of History and the Last Man*. New York: The Free Press.

Giddens, A. (1991) *Modernity and Self-Identity: Self and Society in the Late Modern Age*. Cambridge: Polity Press.

────── (ed.) (1992) *Human Societies: An Introductory Reader in Sociology*. Cambridge: Polity Press.

Hadebe, M.H. (2015) 'Dry City: A history of water problems in Bulawayo, 1980-2014'. BA dissertation, Midlands State University.

Jeater, D. (2012) 'Citizen, Witch or Non-person? Contested Concepts of Personhood in Political Violence and Reconciliation in Zimbabwe, 1978-2008', in D. Kaulemu (ed.) *Imagining Citizenship in Zimbabwe*.

Kaulemu, D. (2004) 'The culture of party politics and the concept of the state', in D. Harold-Barry (ed.) *Zimbabwe: the Past is the Future*. Harare: Weaver Press.

────── (ed.) (2008) 'The Struggles After the Struggle'. Zimbabwean Philosophical Study, 1. Washington, DC: Council for Research in Values and Philosophy.

────── (2011) *Ending Violence in Zimbabwe*. Harare: Konrad-Adenauer-Stiftung in association with the African Forum for Catholic Social Teaching.

────── (ed.) (2012) *Imagining Citizenship in Zimbabwe*. Harare: Konrad-Adenauer-Stiftung in association with the African Forum for Catholic Social Teaching.

Lansley, S. (2012) *The Cost of Inequality: Why Economic Equality is Essential for Recovery*. London, Gibson Square Books.

Mamdani, M. (1996) *Citizen and Subject: Contemporary Africa and the Legacy of Late Colonialism*. Princeton, NJ: Princeton University Press.

Mawowa, S. and E. McCandless (2018) *Unsettled Zimbabwe: The Quest for a Resilient Social Contract*. Harare: Friedrich-Ebert-Stiftung.

Mazarire, G.C. (2009) 'Reflections on Pre-colonial Zimbabwe, c.850-1880s', in B. Raftopoulos and A.S. Mlambo, *Becoming Zimbabwe*.

McLean, G. F. (2005) 'Solidarity and Subsidiarity as the Social Exercise of Human Freedom', in A.F. Perez, S.P. Gueye and F. Yang (eds), *Civil Society as Democratic Practice.* Washington, DC: Council for Research in Values and Philosophy,

Mills, C.W. (1992) 'The Sociological Imagination and the Promise of Sociology', in A. Giddens (ed.) (1992:6) *Human Societies: An Introductory Reader in Sociology.*

────── (2000) *The Sociological Imagination*, with a new Afterword by Todd Gitlin. Oxford: Oxford University Press.

MacIntyre, A (1984) *After Virtue,* 2nd Edition, Notre Dame, University of Notre Dame Press.

Mlambo, A. (2013) 'Becoming Zimbabwe or Becoming Zimbabwean: Identity, Nationalism and State-building', *Afrika Spectrum*, 48(1), pp. 49-70.

Mudenge, S.I. (1988) *A Political History of Munhumutapa. c.1400-1902.* Harare: Zimbabwe Publishing House.

Munochiveyi, M.B. (2011) 'Becoming Zimbabwe From Below: Multiple Narratives of Zimbabwean Nationalism', *Critical African Studies*, 4(6), pp. 84-108.

Ndlovu-Gatsheni, S.J. (2011) 'The Construction and Decline of Chimurenga Monologue in Zimbabwe: A Study in Resilience of Ideology and Limits of Alternatives'. Paper presented at the 4th European Conference on African Studies, Nordic Africa Institute, Uppsala, 15-18 June.

────── (2009) *Do 'Zimbabweans' Exist? Trajectories of Nationalism, Nationall Identity Formation and Crisis in Postcolonial State.* Oxford: Peter Lang.

O'Hear, A. (1985) *What Philosophy is: An Introduction to Contemporary Philosophy*, London: Penguin Books.

Poole, R. (1991) *Morality and Modernity.* London and New York: Routledge.

Pope Benedict XVI (2009) 'Encyclical Letter: Caritas in Veritate'. Rome: Libreria Editrice Vaticana.

Putnam, R.D. (2000) *Bowling Alone: The Collapse and Revival of American* Community. New York: Simon & Schuster.

Quine, W. van O. (1980) 'On what there is', in *From a Logical Point of View: Nine Logico-Philosophical Essays*, Second Revised Edition.

Cambridge, Mass: Harvard University Press.

Raftopoulos, B. and A. Mlambo (eds) (2009) *Becoming Zimbabwe: A History from the Pre-colonial Period to 2008*. Harare: Weaver Press.

Rawls, J. (1971) *A Theory of Justice*. Oxford: Oxford University Press.

Richards, K. and E. Govere (2003) 'Educational Legislation in Colonial Zimbabwe (1899-1979)', *Journal of Educational Administration and History*, 35(2).

Sachikonye, L. (2011) *When a State turns on its Citizens: Institutionalized Violence and Political Culture*. Auckland Park: Jacana Media.

Sachs, J. (2008) *Common Wealth: Economics for a Crowded Planet*. London: Penguin.

Seligman, A.B. (1992) *The Idea of Civil Society*. Princeton, NJ: Princeton University Press.

Sen, A. (1999) *Development as Freedom*. Oxford: Oxford University Press.

Sithole, M. (1979) *Zimbabwe: Struggles within the struggle, 1959-1980*. Salisbury: Rujeko Publishers.

Skillen, A. (1977) *Ruling Illusions: Philosophy and the Social Order*. Hassocks, Sussex: Harvester Press.

Smith, P.B. and M. Max-Neef (2011) *Economics unmasked: from power and greed to compassion and the common good*. Totnes, Devon: Green Books.

Snare, F. (1992) *The Nature of Moral Thinking*. London: Routledge.

Taylor, C. (2004) *Modern Social Imaginaries*. Durham, NC: Duke University Press.

Taylor, C. (1994) 'The Politics of Recognition', in A. Gutman (ed.), *Multiculturalism and the politics of recognition*. Princeton, NJ: Princeton University Press.

Tibaijuka, A.K. (2005) 'Report of the Fact-Finding Mission to Zimbabwe to assess the Scope and Impact of Operation Murambatsvina by the UN Special Envoy on Human Settlements Issues in Zimbabwe'. New York: UNHCS Habitat.

Todd, J.G. 'Citizenship by Birth in Zimbabwe: A Case Study', in D. Kaulemu, *Imagining Citizenship in Zimbabwe*.

UNDP (1990). 'Human Development Report 1990: Concept and

Measurement of Human Development'. New York: UNDP.

UNDP (2004) 'Human Development Report 2004: Cultural Liberty in Today's Diverse World'. New York: UNDP.

West, C. (1993) *Prophetic Thought in Postmodern Times*. Monroe, ME: Common Courage Press.

Zimbabwe Catholic Bishops' Conference (ZCBC) (2020) 'The March is not ended – Pastoral Letter of the Zimbabwe Catholic Bishops' Conference on the current situation in Zimbabwe'. Harare: ZCBC.

3

Elusive development and defective democracy

Lloyd Sachikonye

Introduction

Zimbabwe became 40 in April 2020. This would be a milestone in an individual's life; for a society and nation, it is a birthday that represents a profound landmark. A span of forty years would denote some sense of maturity, durability and stability of a nation, or as some would prefer, a nation-in-the-making. It is a reminder that it will reach its half-century in the not-too-distant future. The fortieth birthday is therefore a major vantage point from which to look back over the past four decades, and look ahead to the next decade.

Zimbabwe began its independent statehood as a middle-income country. It had regressed to become a low-income country by 2020. This chapter is a critical review of Zimbabwe's forty years of evolution and experiences, development and governance.

Zimbabwe is richly endowed with natural resources, yet it has not exploited them to create wealth for the majority of its citizens. This chapter explores the question of why development as broadly understood has proved elusive to Zimbabwe, while its neighbours in Southern Africa have forged ahead. Except for short spurts of dynamic growth in 1980-82 and 2009-2013, the country has either grown very slowly as in the 1980s and 1990s, or regressed, as between 2000 and 2008, and in 2019-2020.

Could the explanation be in the governance system that the country has operated for the past 40 years? Perhaps the structures of authoritarianism and autocracy under the long rule of 37 years under Robert Mugabe and his protégé, Emmerson Mnangagwa, since 2017, provide some reasons or interconnections? Possibly there are broader structural factors and reasons. These are the key questions that we explore in this chapter.

Development in the 1980s

The new government sought economic growth tempered with equity. Its vision of development included expanding employment and raising incomes, promoting rural development and increasing ownership and participation in a significant portion of the economy. An aspect of this development vision was the extension of social services to lower income groups (GoZ 1981).

But how was the question of development itself handled in the first decade of independence? The two key instruments used were the Transitional National Development Plan (TNDP) covering 1982 to 1985, and the First Five-Year National Development Plan (FFYNDP) covering 1986 to 1990. The TNDP spelt out ambitious development targets:

- expanding of linkages within and between manufacturing and other sectors in the economy;
- promotion of import-substitution policies wherever possible;
- decentralisation of industries;
- promotion of labour-intensive industries;
- support for land resettlement of small farmers;
- increase in local participation in the economy (**GOZ 1982**).

The FFYNDP plan sought to achieve an annual growth rate of 5.1%, create 28,000 jobs a year and raise an ambitious US$7 billion investment to be funded 60:40 from domestic and foreign sources respectively.

To what extent did they achieve their objectives? The consensus is that they fell considerably short. For example, the TNDP period mainly registered negative growth in 1982 and 1983 followed by a slight recovery of 1.3% growth in 1984. Employment generation was below target while investment declined over the three-year plan period. By 1985, the volume of investment in fixed assets was one-fifth below its 1982 level, and the share of productive sectors in total investment fell below 40% (Kanyenze et al. 2011: 36).

While growth picked up during the FFYNDP period in 1986-1990, employment grew slowly below target while the budget deficit climbed to about 10% of GDP. How can failure to meet plan targets and development ambitions during the 1980s be explained? The first shortfall was inadequate capacity amongst the new black bureaucrats who had limited knowledge and experience in planning. There was not only a shortage of planners but also a poor understanding of what planning entailed (Stoneman 1988).

There was lack of realism in target setting, and no mechanisms for ensuring compliance with plan targets, and no attempts to use indicative planning techniques to ensure compatibility between objectives. As an example of the lack of real planning, projected growth depended on achieving an export growth rate of 7% per annum without addressing constraints in the domestic economy affecting that growth (Cliffe and Stoneman 1989).

One analyst observed a difference in planning skill levels between the old and new planners: 'the 1980s bureaucrats were not the same breed as the technocrats of the mid-1960s, steeped in monetary and financial interventionism...' (Bond 1998: 183). Colonial bureaucrats had effectively conserved capital to serve the project of Unilateral Declaration of Independence that entailed extensive diversification and import-substitution industrialisation. The new government admitted that there was limited institutional capacity in its ranks, and that weak capacity in line ministries and implementing agencies led to an overstretching of resources devoted to policy analysis and formulation (ibid.: 200). The deficit in development planning skills would continue to haunt the new government in subsequent decades.

A more damning critique of the unrealism in planning and programming was that:

> plans were more matters of elucidating pleasant ends than setting out the means of achieving them...in the absence of mechanisms to implement these, the plans amounted to not much more than elaborations of how paths to the desired ends would look if they occurred, but offered little help with making them occur (Stoneman 1988: 53).

From the TNDP to the ESAP, from ZimAsset to TSP, planning displayed glaring shortfalls and lack of realism. The absence of genuine political will to implement and review plans was conspicuous.

Several trends whose genesis can be traced to the 1980s relate to scarcity of investment flows and the decline in the pre-eminence of manufacturing.

The underlying reason for lack of new investment could be traced to deeper tendencies of stagnation in the productive sectors of the economy, including manufacturing. This made a decisive break with Rhodesian-era structural racism in business and banking extremely difficult (Bond 1998: 164). Both domestic and foreign investment would be insufficient in the next decades, seriously affecting the pace of growth.

A deeper factor limiting investment was insufficient trust in the new government, whose rhetoric about socialist intentions, and later about property rights, did not increase its credibility. Some analysts observed that over-accumulated capital flowed out of the manufacturing sector into financial markets. In the mid-1980s, this tendency was given free rein, contributing to a long-term crisis of stagnation (ibid.: 142). This took the form of stagnation in manufacturing, growth in the financial sector, and the subsequent rise of the World Bank and local financial interests in setting policy in the late 1980s.

We can sum up the factors that derailed the strategies and plans crafted in the 1980s. First, a number of policy blunders were made. Immense pressures were generated as a result of hasty liberalisation of foreign exchange laws. This resulted in outflows of payments and remittances jumping from US$72 million in 1980 to US$206 million in 1982. As a consequence of this policy shift, net foreign assets declined from US$178 million in 1980 to negative levels in 1982, with the debt service ratio increasing three times, to about 30% by 1983 (Kadhani 1986: 108).

In retrospect, the opening of the economy in 1980 exposed it to a hostile global market, raising dependence on the export of primary commodities that tended to be unstable in price. Additional pressures had come from luxury imports such as cars, and a focus on external markets at the cost of failing to develop a strong domestic market in rural areas (Cliffe and Stoneman 1989: 163). To be sure, Zimbabwe's economic elite had regular access to foreign exchange for certain types of luxury consumption; this could have been redirected more rationally to productive investments. There was a contradiction between investment in costly status symbols and need for basic investment in infrastructure and services to generate rural growth.

A valid argument was made that it was not the lack of foreign exchange during the 1980s, but rather the surplus of foreign exchange in the wrong hands and wrong sectors of the economy that most adversely affected the manufacturing industry (Bond 1998: 173). Clearly, some caution would have been necessary before rapid liberalisation was effected soon after independence. While it is possible that the new inexperienced government did not fully understand the consequences, there was subsequently no evidence that useful lessons had been drawn from this type of policy mistake in later years. At the same time, the influence of the leading technocrat, Dr. Bernard Chidero, who was a Minister of Finance for over 10 years, was considerable in the shift toward neo-liberal economic policies.

Second, the lack of clarity on industrial strategy was another weakness in the 1980s. The coordinating capacity of the state left much to be desired, especially in defining an industrial policy. The overall development strategy of the 1980s was one based on what was termed the least common denominator of radical and reformist proposals for development (Gordon 1984: 128).

There was clearly tension between investments in social services and those in industrial and infrastructural sectors. By committing the government to relatively heavy spending in social services, recurrent expenditures skyrocketed. Investment in education and health for social development was necessary and politically popular, but a balance was necessary. The avoiding of hard choices exacerbated the problem, meaning that the 'cost of avoiding political conflict was the loss of control over expenditures' (ibid.).

By the end of the 1980s, a template had been drawn that would influence policy flip-flops in later decades. These included weak policy towards industrialisation, perpetual shortage of foreign exchange, meagre foreign investment, state impediments to the growth of a black bourgeoisie, and the absence of a coordinated developmental role by the state. Discussed in sections below, these challenges and gaps would feature in later decades together with corruption and predatory tendencies.

Development in the early 1990s: the switch to structural adjustment

The recourse to adjustment in Zimbabwe's second decade of independence was an admission by the Mugabe administration that its development strategy in the 1980s had not been successful. Government debt had reached 71% of GDP by 1989, of which 36% was external (GoZ 1991). As we observed above, private sector investment remained low at 10% of GDP. High fiscal deficit and a tightly regulated business environment deterred investors. Export growth at 3.4% per annum between 1980 and 1989 coupled with debt service repayments severely constrained the growth of imports. This in turn undermined utilisation of existing capacity and re-equipment of plants. A continuation of the policies of the 1980s was unlikely to generate sustainable growth, and achieve such a development transition as had occurred in newly industrialised countries like those in East Asia.

The economic structural adjustment programme (ESAP) was a five-year conventional stabilisation programme with some features that promised trade and investment growth, as we observed above. For instance, it promised budget deficit reduction, fiscal and monetary reforms, trade liberalisation, deregulation of investment, labour and price controls as well as public enterprise reforms (including privatisation) (GoZ 1991: 4). Equally ambitious was the programme's intention to eliminate direct subsidies and transfers to public enterprises by 1995.

Under ESAP, a process of trade liberalisation would be instituted to move from a state-administered, forex-based system to a market-based one. This measure and others were expected to contribute to greater investment inflows that were projected to rise to 25% of GDP by 1995. Furthermore, the adjustment process would aim at the creation of 100,000 new jobs in the formal sector between 1992 and 1995.

Although ESAP was sold as a 'home-grown' adjustment programme, the policy intervention and financing by the World Bank and IMF were considerable. Financing largely depended on the level of progress made in the implementation of the programme. However, most targets were not achieved. Some analysts observed that GDP grew at about 1% from 1991 to 1995 while inflation averaged more than 30% (Bond and Manyanya 2003: 32). Meanwhile, the budget deficit had remained stubbornly high at more than 10% during the ESAP period.

Most indicators pointed to a failure of ESAP adjustment measures. For instance, one analyst summarised the shortfalls as punitive interest rates, contraction in foreign investment, a speculative surge in imports, and technically deficient implementation owing to poor plan design (Gibbon 1995: 13). A major drought in 1992 threatened to derail ESAP because of significant food imports. Contingency planning had not been integral to the programme. On the whole, ESAP was distinguished for missing its many targets, and exposing the weakness of the adjustment model as a development strategy.

A study commissioned by the national labour centre, Zimbabwe Congress of Trade Unions (ZCTU), observed that the immediate combined effect of ESAP and the 1992 drought had been stagflationary (ZCTU 1996: 14). To deal with inflationary pressures, monetary policy was tightened by keeping the rediscount rate high, with adverse consequences on private sector demand for credit. Central government debt more than tripled from Z$11 billion in 1990 to about Z$41 billion in 1995, while external debt rose from 41% to 52% by 1995.

Formal sector employment declined instead of expanding during ESAP. Employment in the non-agricultural sector declined from 940,000 in 1991 to 844,000 in 1992 with many private sector employers shedding permanent employees in preference for casual workers (ibid.: 15). By 1995, scores of thousands of workers had been retrenched from the public and private sectors. There was also a marked decline in real wages for the majority of workers.

In sum, the demand-reducing consequences of the stabilisation measures under ESAP had far outweighed the anticipated supply response (ibid.). The stagflationary outcome was a consequence of the inability of the Mugabe administration to restructure expenditures and rein in the budget deficit. The discipline to manage the national budget would be a recurrent challenge to the administration as it sought to avoid the political consequences of reducing social expenditure and the public sector workforce. The lack of management discipline occurred in a context of rising social demands for access to education, health and rural development and restrictive policy prescriptions from the IFIs during ESAP. In the final analysis, as we observe later, the instinct for political self-preservation through power retention at all costs proved stronger in situations that required such discipline.

In its evaluation, the World Bank was candid enough to concede the unsatisfactory outcome of ESAP. In particular, the failure to properly sequence trade liberalisation, and other measures such as setting up conditions for rapid expansion of exports early on, placed many domestic firms at a disadvantage and delayed the supply response (World Bank 1995:11). This newly found wisdom on the part of the World Bank was an attribute of hindsight for it had been originally dogmatic about the need for a 'big bang' approach to stabilisation and adjustment. However, as in similar cases elsewhere of adjustment programmes gone wrong, it was the implementing government, not the IFIs, that picked up the tab for the expensive blunders.

The Zimbabwe Government was not agile or flexible enough to modify policy measures during the implementation of adjustment. For example, it was clear halfway through ESAP that many manufacturing firms were operating at a disadvantage in an uneven playing field of increased external competition while carrying a burden of tax, tariff and regional trade anomalies (ibid.). The net result of these anomalies was a much-weakened manufacturing sector by the mid-1990s.

With a few exceptions, state enterprises did not perform to expectation during ESAP. In 1994, the operating deficit of nine major enterprises amounted to 3.3% of GDP, while in 1995 the government inherited parastatal debts amounting to Z$4 billion. Persistent lacklustre performance and large losses weighed heavily on public finances and would continue to drain state coffers in later decades.

The failure of economic reform has been attributed to several factors. Perhaps the most realistic assessment was that failure was due to a combination of both technical and political factors. Technically, implementation of reform was poor. For their part, ESAP programme designers misread and misunderstood the political environment in which they were operating (Simpson and Hawkins 2018). The designers assumed wrongly that politicians were committed to reform when in fact they were more interested in maintaining their monopoly on power than in pursuing development.

2000 to 2020: the lost development decades

If the first and second decades experienced unimpressive stewardship of the development process, the two decades beginning 2000 would witness contraction and decline followed by stop-start growth. As the authoritarian Mugabe administration dug in, the economy began to shrink precipitously. Perhaps the two biggest factors that dealt a blow to the economy, and therefore the development process broadly, were the fast track land reform, and the creation of hyperinflationary conditions in a context of declining investor confidence.

Fast track land reform was a knee-jerk response to loss of a referendum vote in 2000, and commercial farmers' support for the newly formed MDC party. This is not to argue that land reform was not overdue. Highlighting the centrality of the land question, some sporadic land occupations spearheaded by small farmers had occurred in 1998 in Masvingo and Mashonaland East provinces. But some semblance of order had been restored subsequently before the comprehensive land invasions from 2000.

Our focus in this chapter is not so much on the narrative of the trajectory of the Fast Track Land Reform programme (FTLRP) but on its ramifications on the economy. The disruptive impact of FTLRP has not been given the scholarly attention that it deserves. The lack of planning in how land reform could create linkages and synergies with manufacturing and other sectors robbed the country of a major opportunity for a development transition. Elsewhere, we observed that in the absence of land reform that supported the growth of an agro-industry creating many jobs, and of increased linkages between agriculture and industry, there was little likelihood of a successful industrial transition (Sachikonye 2012: 96). There was no strategy within the FTLRP to systematically nurture and maintain the agriculture-industry interconnections that had been built over many decades.

Policy makers missed an opportunity to set these linkages on a sustainable path by drawing more small farmers into production and promoting diversification into small and medium-sized industries. The opportunity to enlarge the domestic market for various inputs such as seed, fertiliser, equipment, irrigation materials and consumer goods amongst smallholders were missed in the 1980s and 1990s. So was this opportunity to extend and consolidate backward and forward linkages between industry and smallholder agriculture in the 2000s. This would have been one path to break the dualism that had been embedded in the Zimbabwean economy and society since colonialism.

For latter-day land reformers, it is astounding that the planning of good practices in agriculture-industry linkages was not of the highest priority. It was not as if there had not been the belief in some quarters that increased demand in agriculture for industrial goods would result in an expansion of output in the manufacturing sector. This would have increased profits and savings to spur further expansion (ZCTU 1996:17). The supply of cheap wage goods in the form of food and raw materials from the rural sector would lower costs of production in the industrial sector, and reinforce productivity and output expansion. The increased demand for goods in rural areas would be used as an opportunity to promote decentralisation of industry to smaller towns and growth points. A symbiotic relationship between the two sectors would be strengthened while steadily reducing dualism.

At the outset of land reform, over half of inputs into agriculture were supplied by the manufacturing sector, while in the reverse direction some 44% of agricultural output was sold to that sector. Of the latter, over 94% was supplied by the commercial farming sector, and the balance by small producers (Simpson and Hawkins 2018: 110). Inevitably, during the FTLR programme, the disarticulation of these linkages and their ripple effects were felt widely and rapidly in the economy. For instance, between 2000 and 2008, value added in manufacturing declined by 62% (ibid.). While most focus was on the amount of land that was acquired for distribution – and it was impressive by any standards – the qualitative social and economic consequences for the largely agro-based economy were missed or minimised in the discourse on reform.

The economy was shaken to its core by the land disruptions, and would take decades to recover:

> [O]n the cost side, not only was there the damage done to the economy as a result of the severing of previously symbiotic linkages between agriculture and industry, a rupturing that was a significant contributor to the negative growth rates of the crisis decade, but also a weakening of the institutional fabric that will take decades to repair (ibid.: 99).

The ramifications of this collapse of production are still playing out some two decades later.

For the remainder of the economy, the 2000s were like a roller coaster. Not only did it shrink by over 40% by 2008, it experienced a combination of acute shortages of key inputs such as electricity, fuel and fertiliser. Foreign exchange scarcity exacerbated the shortages to the detriment of the economy. Hyperinflation was rampant in the 2000s; from 57% in 1999, it accelerated to over 1,000% in 2006 before climbing to 231 million per cent in September 2008 (Kanyenze 2018: 82). Economic instability was compounded by ad hoc measures such as ther quasi-fiscal operations of the Reserve Bank of Zimbabwe.

In economic policy design and implementation during the 2000s, the political factor loomed large. One survey observed that:

> political imperatives took precedence over economic goals... in exchange rate policy and pricing policies of parastatals... Economic policies seem to have been driven by the need to secure immediate and medium-term goals, while paying scant attention to collateral

social and economic consequences of such actions (UNDP 2008: 211).

It appeared that economic decisions and programmes formulated after 2000 had the primary rationale of prolonging ZANU-PF's stay in office. The Mugabe administration's overall objective was to avoid what was colloquially termed 'regime change'. Sensing its vulnerability in forthcoming elections, it deployed two instruments: extensive patronage that consisted of material incentives to retain its supporters and buy votes, and coercion against opposition supporters. In such a context, there was little likelihood of rational economic policies with a medium- and long-term perspectives. Even though a number of plans were drawn up, there was clearly little political will for their implementation.

In the absence of medium and long-term planning, the Mugabe administration resorted to ad hoc crisis management of the economy in the 2000s. In reality, the annual budget became the principal instrument of economic policy during this decade. Ministers of Finance often had short tenure as the President sought greater influence on economic policy and national budget process. Not only were the above-mentioned shortages symptoms of the depth of the crisis, but so also were basic consumer goods scarcities. There emerged thriving parallel markets for basic commodities where prices were much higher than controlled prices. Ironically, the beneficiaries of price controls had turned out to be 'speculators and dealers, and not targeted vulnerable groups' (GoZ 2002: 14).

The ripple effects of the crisis included the production of lower quality goods as producers were forced to 'shave' inputs in order to maintain profit margins, and loss of employment opportunities as companies downsized production. There was an increasing resort to informal methods of economic transactions such as barter trade, and the mortgaging of natural resources to countries including China and Libya in opaque deals.

This was the context in which Gideon Gono was appointed as Governor of the Reserve Bank of Zimbabwe in 2003, and he soon usurped the powers and authority normally wielded by a Minister of Finance. The RBZ showed disdain for conventional methods of economic management, which were often derisively dismissed as 'textbook or bookish economics'. Its interventionism was justified in these terms:

> where a national economy experiences real, persistent and

unprecedented structural shocks and where those shocks transform the market economy into a bubble-driven casino economy as happened in Zimbabwe from 2000 to 2008, monetary policy must then necessarily do more by getting out of the traditional mandate toolbox in order to take into account the contextual factors on the ground from a pragmatic point of view (Gono 2008: 139).

Table 1: Zimbabwe's Economic Programmes, 1991-2020

Economic Structural Adjustment Programme (ESAP) 1991-1995	An adjustment programme that involved stabilisation and reforms
Zimbabwe Economic Programme for Social and Economic Transformation (ZIMPREST) 1996	A follow-up adjustment programme that was stillborn
Millennium Economic Recovery Programme (MERP) 2001	A recovery programme that ran concurrently with the Millennium Budget
National Economic Revival Programme (NERP) 2003	A 12-month stabilisation programme
National Economic Development Priority Programme (NEDPP) 2007	A short-term but ineffective recovery programme
Zimbabwe Economic Development Strategy (ZEDS) 2008	A still-born economic strategy
Short-Term Emergency Recovery Programme 1 (STERP 1) 2009	A short-term recovery programme under the GNU
Short-term Emergency Recovery Programme (STERP 11) 2009-2011	Also implemented under the GNU as a macro-economic policy and budget framework
Medium term Plan (MTP) 2011-2013	A medium term plan under the GNU
Zimbabwe Agenda for Sustainable Socio-Economic Transformation (ZimAsset) 2013-2018	Implemented by a ZANU-PF majority government
Transitional Stabilisation Programme 2018-2020	A stabilisation programme designed and implemented under the Mnangagwa government

Source: GoZ (various programmes, 1991-2018)

Gono defined the mission of RBZ as adopting a deliberate policy to stimulate productive economic activities by providing concessional funding to key sectors, most notably agriculture. This meant devising 'extraordinary and innovative measures and interventions to stimulate economic activity, ensure food self-sufficiency, stabilise energy supplies, arrest further decline and rein inflation' (ibid. 145).

Table 2: RBZ Quasi-Fiscal Programmes, 2003-2007 Scheme Purpose

Productive Sector Finance Facility in 2003	to assist firms in various sectors to boost production
Agricultural Sector Productivity Enhancement Facility (ASPEF) in 2005	to resuscitate the agricultural sector
Parastatals and Local Authorities Reorientation Programme (PLARP) in 2005	to remove structural and supply rigidities
Troubled Bank Fund in 2003	to assist distressed and solvent banking institutions with temporary liquidity support
Basic Commodities Supply-Side Intervention Facility (BACOSSI) in 2007	To assist producers and suppliers in specific sectors to have access to concessional production-linked financial support for working capital requirements

Source: Gono 2008.

The RBZ thus placed itself at the centre of virtually all major activities in the economy. It printed money and pumped resources into ailing sectors such as agriculture, parastatals and local authorities; it extended support for health services, including the fight against the 2008 cholera outbreak, and provided basic commodities for rural and urban communities under the Basic Commodities Supply-Side Intervention programme (ibid.). Although they required significant resources, these quasi-fiscal activities spearheaded by the RBZ were not a permanent solution to the decline.

The GNU interlude

The formation of a Government of National Unity (GNU) in 2009 was a consequence of an electoral impasse in which the opposition MDC-T and MDC won a parliamentary majority, and Mugabe retained the presidency after a violent run-off in 2008. Brokered by Thabo Mbeki, the GNU proved an economic and political lifeline for the Mugabe administration and an almost bankrupt economy. Under the tutelage of a capable Finance Minister, Tendai Biti, the economy not only recovered but also grew respectably between 2009 and 2013. This was achieved under a short-term emergency recovery programme that sought to stabilise the economy, and to recover levels of savings, investment and growth (GoZ 2009: paragraph 6). More broadly, it sought to lay a basis for a more transformative medium- to long-term economic programme to turn Zimbabwe into a developmental state.

The economy responded positively to stimulus, dollarisation and a more disciplined stewardship during this GNU phase. GDP grew by 5.4% in 2009, by 11% in 2010, by 11.9% in 2011 and by 10.6% in 2012. This dramatic recovery was buoyed by the mining sector, which with high global prices became the leading export sector ahead of agriculture (Kanyenze 2018: 86). Inflation fell to 3.7% in 2012, and investment flows improved. There was a rise of confidence during the GNU period in the context of dollarisation, and the reining in of government profligacy that had been a feature reflecting Mugabe's instincts.

However, the GNU interlude was short, and ZANU-PF sustained its previous habits of profligacy through creation of parallel income streams outside the national budget. Revenues from diamonds that had been discovered at Marange in eastern Zimbabwe in mid-2000s were diverted into ZANU-PF's coffers and military-linked companies. As some analysts observed:

> the exploitation of diamond resources rapidly led to the country displaying all the features of the resource curse syndrome. ZANU-PF grasped the potential for diamond revenues to be used to meet the needs of a ZANU-PF parallel government. Those needs ranged from self-enrichment by the military and the politically well connected to the financing of party political campaigns and state controlled media, and its support base of war veterans, youth militia and traditional leaders (Simpson and Hawkins 2018: 211).

Hopes by the Finance Minister of receiving tax revenues of around US$600 million from diamond sales in 2010 to 2012 were dashed. Instead, the Treasury only received US$41 million, a revealing indication of the magnitude of leakages, and sophistication of the parallel revenue generating systems set up during the GNU.

That the recovery could not be sustained was quickly revealed when the GNU ended in 2013 with ZANU-PF's landslide victory. With a two-thirds parliamentary majority, ZANU-PF could afford to ignore the opposition. However, such restraint as there was in competent economic management evaporated with the Mugabe administration assuming power again in 2013 to steer economic policy. What the Biti era of economic management under GNU had demonstrated was that it was possible to create a turnaround in development provided the relevant toolbox of measures was judiciously applied. Even so, this was a fragile recovery because the 'greatest lesson from Zimbabwe was the danger of subordinating economic policies to political expediency' (Biti 2015: 22). This was what resumed after the 2013 election victory of ZANU-PF.

The post-2013 economic downturn

Economic policies in the aftermath of the election signalled a return to the overspending and opaque dealings within the Mugabe administration. Restraint was removed with a return to rampant patronage that fuelled expenditure and flip-flop policies that discouraged investment. Like before, an ambitious development plan was hastily cobbled together in 2013. Termed the Zimbabwe Agenda for Sustainable Socio-Economic Transformation (ZimAsset), the plan sought to provide a framework for steering the economy during the following five years. It was based on four strategic clusters: (1) food security and nutrition; (2) social services and poverty reduction; (3) infrastructure and utilities and (4) value addition and beneficiation (GoZ 2013). As in previous plans, there was no realistic funding and implementation path mapped out.

Analysts argued that with regard to ZimAsset funding, the administration showed 'signs of collective amnesia and apparent economic illiteracy against a backdrop of ZANU-PF's track record of economic mismanagement' (Simpson and Hawkins 2018: 343). This was exemplified by expansionary and opaque spending that followed. Economic growth slowed down in the 2014 to 2018 period. In addition, international commodity prices were also weakening with negative effects on export receipts. There was a return to the high budget deficits of the 2000s. From 0.1% in 2012, the deficit rose to about 10% in 2017.

The priority for the Mugabe administration seemed to be to ensure that resources were flowing again in accordance with its regime maintenance objectives. In 2016, the administration returned to the lavish printing of 'bond notes' that were reminiscent of the bearer cheques that it printed in the 2000s. There was a new burst of dirigisme in the RBZ's return to quasi-fiscal activities. In 2016, some supplementary spending for fuel, fertiliser, machinery and spares, wheat and grain was only possible through such quasi-fiscal activities. As it was pointed out:

> while the country experienced fiscal surpluses during most of the GNU period as a result of strict adherence to cash budgeting and fiscal discipline, after 2013 the spectre of fiscal indiscipline re-emerged, reminiscent of the previous decade (Kanyenze 2018: 95).

Significant spending followed with massive resources poured into what was termed the 'Command Agriculture' programme. There was resort to issuing of Treasury Bills and RBZ overdrafts for these expenditures.

By 2017, the economy was under massive stress. GDP growth slumped from 4.5% in 2013 to 0.7% in 2016. The contribution of state-owned enterprises to the economy had declined precipitously from around 60% to 2%, with 70% of the enterprises technically insolvent (ibid.). The level of debt was also a source of economic difficulty. It amounted to an estimated US$11 billion, or 79% of GDP, of which about US$7 billion was external debt (ibid.: 100). Attempts to negotiate with IFIs for better repayment terms were futile. Foreign investment inflows fell to a trickle during this period.

A major attempt at an economic shift was the Transitional Stabilisation Programme (TSP) in 2018 following the election of Emmerson Mnangagwa as president, and the appointment of Mthuli Ncube as Finance Minister. Presented as a version of 'shock therapy' reminiscent of ESAP, implemented 18 years earlier with painful outcomes, the TSP promised economic deliverance within two years. It was promised that:

> the realisation of the TSP short-term quick-wins for the economy will be underpinned by the adoption of, and strict adherence to, macroeconomic stabilisation policies that require painful trade-off and sacrifice. This is necessary to address fundamental challenges besetting the economy over the immediate term (GoZ 2018: 7).

In addition, it was also pledged that government would undertake significant reforms such as ease of doing business and opening the country to international investors and financiers. The economy was projected to grow at about 9% from 2019 to 2022 (ibid.: 8). As in previous plans, this was an overly ambitious target that bore little resemblance to the realities in the country. In 2018, the economy only grew by 3.4% against a target of 6.3%, while in 2019 it declined by -6.5% against a target of 9%.[1] In 2020,

---

[1] 'A review of the Transitional Stabilisation Programme', *Zimbabwe Independent*, 21 August 2020.

partly due to the COVID-19 pandemic, it is projected to decline by -10% against an ambitious target of 9.7%.

Zimbabwe: Real GDP Trends, 2000-2019 (%)

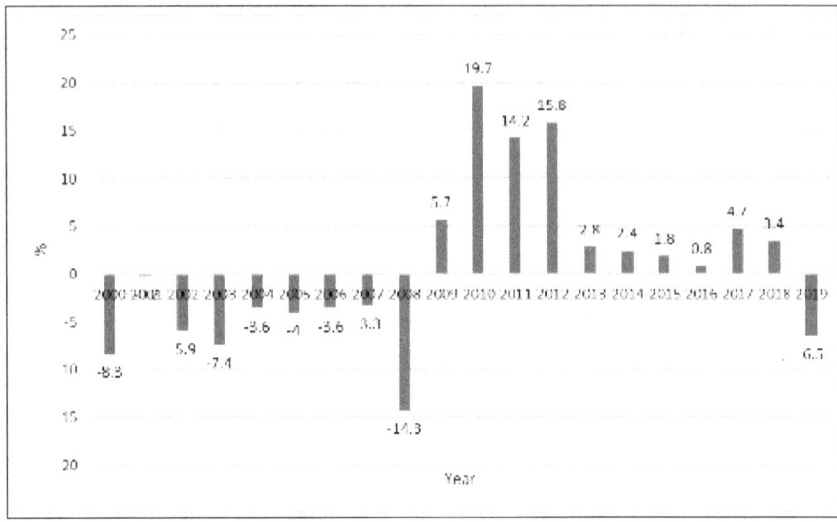

Source: G. Kanyenze as derived from data from Ministry of Finance & Economic Development.

During the next two years, there was indeed considerable pain and sacrifice. There was a huge devaluation of the Zimbabwe dollar introduced in mid-2019. Incomes were slashed in real terms, while the cost of living skyrocketed. Industry encountered heavy knocks in a context of endless shortages of inputs and foreign exchange. By mid-2020, hyperinflation had reached about 785%.

This assessment of the trajectory of development since 1980 would not be complete without some consideration of the structural changes in the economy. Drawing on observations of a respected economist, we can note the following:

- The contribution of agriculture to total output declined from an average of 20% during the period 1997-2008 to 10% during 2009-2016; agriculture exports which were 44% of the total in 1999 had declined to 29% in 2017;

- Manufacturing's contribution to total output dwindled from 21% in 1980 to 8.5% in 2016 while manufactured exports which peaked at 41.4% in 2003 plummeted to 9.5% in 2017;

- The mining sector's contribution increased from 5.8% in 1997-2008 to 7.5% during 2009-2016 (Kanyenze 2018: 103).

This evidence suggests that Zimbabwe had become a typical Sub-Saharan African economy based on primary commodity exports where agriculture and mining accounted for 88% of exports in 2017. 'Instead of enjoying a "structural bonus" associated with industrialisation, Zimbabwe instead had experienced a structural regression' (ibid.).

4. Entitlement, corruption and rent seeking

The sense of entitlement to state-based resources by ruling elites deepened in the 2000s. Several factors combined to consolidate this corruption-linked entitlement. The first related to the acquisition of land, without paying for it, during the fast track land reform in 2000. In one of the largest episodes of land reform, millions of hectares exchanged hands while about 4,000 white commercial farmers were sent packing. Land acquisition by black occupiers was justified in terms of repossession of lands expropriated at the beginning of colonisation, and the new laws introduced from 2000 to consolidate the transfer. The sweeping land take-overs opened the sluice gates for corrupt dealings.

In the absence of transparency, the land reform process came to be riddled with corrupt tendencies. For instance, there was ownership of multiple farms by the powerful elite, contrary to the one-person one-farm official policy. As an analyst observed:

> … when rude power is directing an accumulation strategy, contested meanings are found between conventions of property ownership that would see these acts as theft supported by violence, and a normative of restitution within the paradigm of patriotic nationalism where the acquisition of property from the rich whites is legitimated… (Bracking 2009; see also Utete Report 2003).

Clearly, the primary accumulation of land at little or no cost was a form of 'accumulation by dispossession'. It is arguable that the entire process was an instance of corruption, a process in which any resemblance of morality, justice and fairness was compromised. That the process gave momentum to widespread corruption as evidenced by Mugabe's family amassing more than ten farms is generally clear. The process has also been termed the 'spoils of the politics of accumulation' in which seizure of resources by an elite is viewed as non-cash payment for status. Since 2000, the state has used land as a resource to dispense patronage, and also used its seizure as a punitive measure against owners who challenge the ruling party politically.

The second arena in which corruption became institutionalised was the parastatals. The number of state-owned enterprises (SOEs) increased sharply from about 20 at independence to 76 in the 2000s (UNDP 2008:186). Created in multiple sectors, they were expected to generate profit or at least to break even. That has not been the case with the majority of them. Their internal processes of recruitment, promotion and remuneration of senior staff depended on loyalty to the ruling party rather than competence. SOEs were soon viewed as 'gold mines' by their chief operating officers.

Salaries and allowances reached staggering levels for SOE management in the post-2000 period. In the GNU period, drawing on US-denominated salaries and allowances pegged to earlier Z$ levels, and regardless of the performance, the executives were amongst the highest paid earners in the economy. The most notorious case was that of the CEO of the Public Service Medical Aid Society (PSMAS) who took home US$500,000 every month (TIZ 2014). Some continued to pay inflated salaries while their low-level workers went for months without pay; others, such as Air Zimbabwe and National Railways of Zimbabwe, reduced their service to skeletal levels due to haemorrhage of their resources. These were cases of combined dysfunctionality and corruption.

Table 3: Monthly Salaries and Benefits of State Owned Enterprises CEOs

Name	CEO's Salary US$	CEO's Benefits US$	Monthly Total US$
Public Service Medical Aid Society (PSMAS)	230,030	305,499	535,499
NETONE	10,126	33,567	43,693
Zimbabwe Broadcasting Corporation (ZBC)	15,030	22,050	37,080
Infrastructure Development Bank of Zimbabwe (IDBZ)	18,502	16,944	35,446

Name	CEO's Salary	CEO's Benefits	Monthly Total
National Social Security Authority (NSSA)	13,328	15,824	29,152
Zimbabwe Mining Development Corporation (ZMDC)	13,744	17,978	31,978

Source: TIZ (2014)

No less an institution than the RBZ expressed anxiety and discomfiture about the rising levels of corruption in the early 2000s. Box 1 below provides a list of the main forms of corruption in 2005 as diagnosed by the RBZ. As we observed earlier, between 2003 and 2008 it played an uncharacteristic interventionist role that overshadowed the Ministry of Finance. However, this did not prevent the RBZ from shady interventions that fanned corruption itself. Some of the interventions involved use of public resources in politically oriented measures that mobilised significant funds without adequate targeting, management, accounting and monitoring mechanisms.

From the extensive interventions, not only the public sector but the private sector as well was drawn into a web that was not immunised against corruption. No sooner had these various programmes and funds been established by the RBZ than loopholes were exploited for self-enrichment and aggrandisement by politicians, bureaucrats and businessmen (Gono 2008).

The political system and the ruling 'civil-military coalition'

What are the principal features of the political system in which the rise and decline in economic development has occurred in the past 40 years? What bearing has the system had on the trajectory and tempo of the development process? A survey of Zimbabwe's development experience would be incomplete without assessing how the political system has evolved and shaped thinking about development.

Box 1 Select Forms of Corruption, 2005

1. Payment of bribes to law enforcement agents by fugitives in order to have their economic and other forms of crimes quashed.
2. Payment of bribes by traders – individual and corporate – to ZIMRA officials for underpayment of taxes and import duties, as well as under-invoicing of export shipments.
3. Misrepresentation of facts by some Ministers with the effect of misdirecting public opinion and sentiment, which in turn created a false sense of security, particularly in the food and energy sectors.
4. Outright diversion of resources from purposes for which they were provided into own use. This included productive sector funds, foreign exchange, and other support in kind such as machinery and equipment, which was being diverted to kick-backs and bribes.
5. Smuggling of precious minerals and basic commodities including sugar, grain, cooking oil and soap, which are sold into regional economies on the strength of bribes being paid to inspectorate arms of government to turn a blind eye to the leakages.
6. Flouting of tender procedures and biased awarding of contracts to suppliers and contractors on the back of patronage, kick-backs and bribes.
7. Patronising and wasteful publicity and advertisement campaigns by parastatal and municipal sectors aimed at swaying government policy into condoning their under-performance.
8. Nepotism in key sectors and institutions where efficiency norms were set aside for considerations other than productive efficiency.
9. Insider dealing, for instance on the Stock Exchange, as well as 'interested party effects' on formulation of key government policies such as the setting of producer prices.

Source: RBZ (2005): 10-12

In the 1980s, the political framework was defined by the Lancaster House constitution that provided for a parliamentary system under a prime minister and a ceremonial president until 1987. It was a framework that permitted opposition parties to thrive in an electoral system that required regular elections. This formal side of the political system could be described as a type of competitive authoritarianism. In such an system:

> ... although elections are regularly held...incumbents routinely abuse state resources, deny the opposition adequate media coverage, harass opposition candidates and their supporters and in some cases manipulate electoral results (Levitsky and Way 2002:2).

ZANU-PF, the largest party in parliament, soon accumulated significant powers and control over state institutions, including the security forces and the broadcast media.

Although a nominally democratic system was installed, it quickly came under pressure as a consequence of a civil war in the Matabeleland provinces and parts of Midlands between 1982 and 1987. The military and other security forces were deployed and up to 20,000 people, mostly civilians, were killed in a conflict that left a residue of bitterness and trauma (CCJPZ and LRF 1997). That turmoil during the first decade gave impetus to the inception of authoritarian and militaristic tendencies that would grow in latter decades. This broad trend was not slowed by the merger between ZANU-PF and PF ZAPU parties in a Unity Accord in 1987.

By the close of the 1980s, Zimbabwe had adopted a presidential system with Robert Mugabe inaugurated as executive president in 1987. Exercising extensive powers, augmented by some constitutional amendments in later years, allowed him to accumulate more authority. However, it is debatable whether a powerful presidency necessarily resulted in better governance. Indeed, rumblings of political discontent against corruption were heard as early as during the 1990 election campaign.

From the mid-1990s, stirrings of opposition from civil society against the growth of authoritarianism began to change the political atmosphere and the tone of debates. In particular, the labour movement grew to become the focus of social and economic protests during and after ESAP, whose austerity was painfully felt far and wide. A movement, the National Constitutional Assembly (NCA), was founded in 1997 to advocate for popular participation in constitutional reform. These stirrings were a harbinger of a broader political movement against Mugabe's autocratic tendencies.

As we observed elsewhere, the trajectory of authoritarianism had long-term repercussions on intra-party democracy, inter-party relations, and more broadly, on political values (Sachikonye 2017). A tendency toward intolerance and a propensity to use violence against political opponents became defining features of post-independence politics in Zimbabwe. To this intolerance was added a proclivity toward a personality cult around Robert Mugabe. As a consequence, instead of a nationalism imbued with broad democratic values and practice, a resilient variety of authoritarianism emerged.

The correlated political culture reflected a drift toward intolerance, exclusivity, authoritarianism and violence. The emphasis that nationalism placed on unity at all costs – and the concurrent subordination of organisations such as trade unions and churches to this imperative – gave rise to intolerance and a shift to a 'commandist' state (Ranger 2003).

In addition to nationalism, the experience of the liberation struggle between 1964 and 1979 had a profoundly lasting effect on the outlook of the ruling elite. Two key factors reflected this. The first was the belief that resolving political questions was the exclusive domain of the liberation movement. The second was a strong notion of entitlement to holding political power. An additional impediment to the establishment of a democratic polity has been authoritarian militarism, a major characteristic of the liberation movement. Scant attention to individual and civic rights was exacerbated by a context in which the liberation process itself was fraught with intense intrigues, factionalism and violent purges. The liberation war itself was significant in other respects:

> [I]t gave birth to a coalition in which civilian and military elements were in periodic tension over political leadership … a tense atmosphere encouraged a polarized outlook among leaders in which the political world was starkly divided between a small circle of trusted confidantes and a hostile landscape full of implacable enemies (Bratton 2014: 28).

The ZANU-PF party and state leadership in the post-independence period used the sacrifices made during the liberation process as the ultimate justification for their own political and economic entitlement. As liberators, they claimed to own Zimbabwe in the fullest sense of the word, namely that the country belonged to them, and to no one else. For longer-term significance, they traced political legitimacy not to universal political liberties and open elections:

> whose procedures, results and validity they readily dismiss, but to an armed victory in a liberation war. Thus the leaders of a vanguard party has won not only a right to rule in perpetuity; they are also

entitled to seize the nation's wealth as they see fit (ibid.).

This largely explains why political and military leaders are among the wealthiest in Zimbabwe's ruling elite.

As in other countries that underwent armed liberation in Southern Africa, there was a process of fusion of the ruling party and the state in Zimbabwe. This took the form of party cadres being appointed to key positions in state institutions, ranging from the civil service to the military and state-owned enterprises. There was a strong belief that the party was superior to the institutions of government: ministers and civil servants received orders from the ruling party. Articulating this position, Mugabe claimed that ZANU-PF was more important than the government, and that the Central Committee was above the Cabinet 'because ministers derive their power from ZANU-PF... in the future, there will be no separation of the party from state organs'.[2] The structure of the Zimbabwean party-state system made it difficult to disentangle it, still less to ensure accountability and transparency in state institutions.

The party-state structure developed various centres of power; some revolved around factions of the ruling party and some around the Presidency itself. The balance of power and influence between the different factions became unstable in the post-2013 period as Mugabe became advanced in age, and his spouse emerged as a major political player in her own right. Earlier in the 2000s, the two main factions in ZANU-PF coalesced around Solomon Mujuru and Emmerson Mnangagwa, who both possessed unassailable liberation war credentials, amassed considerable wealth over the years, and had extensive networks in the military and intelligence forces.

The contest between the two factions sharpened in the build-up to the 2008 election and afterwards. The Mujuru faction was suspected of being lukewarm in its support for Mugabe's re-election, and was believed to have surreptitiously backed Simba Makoni's presidential bid. Mugabe countered this by appointing Mnangagwa as chair of the increasingly powerful Joint Operations Command (JOC) that spearheaded the run-off election campaign in which a great deal of violence was meted out against the opposition MDC-T. Subsequently, Mnangagwa was appointed Defence Minister, while the Mujuru faction was marginalised. The fortunes of the Mujuru faction suffered a permanent blow with his suspicious death in a

---

2   Quoted on ZBC News, 18 February 1984.

fire in 2011, and the sacking of Joyce Mujuru as Vice-President in 2014.

The early 2000s appeared to have been a turning point in the attitude of the military towards political power. Abandoning professionalism and a non-partisan approach, the military openly declared its support for Mugabe in the 2002 election:

> [W]e [the JOC] wish to make it very clear to all Zimbabweans that the security organizations will only stand in support of those political leaders that will pursue Zimbabwean values, traditions and beliefs for which thousands of lives were lost in pursuit of Zimbabwe's hard-won independence, sovereignty and national interests.[3]

In a show of assertiveness, the JOC warned that the presidency was 'a straightjacket' whose occupant was expected to observe the objectives of the liberation struggle.

In the 2008 election, the military became the 'kingmakers' when Mugabe lost during the first round; it is widely believed that the military played an active role during the second round that was riddled with considerable violence. By agreeing to be installed by the military in 2008, Mugabe became beholden to it in future.

The drift towards a military state henceforth became more explicit. An authoritarian development path in which the military was a major player was envisaged. Having restored Mugabe's fortunes through campaigning and violence, the military was proved to have the capacity to be a kingmaker, and potentially to become 'king' itself in the future.

In sum, in this militarised 'deep state' some structures are more powerful than others. Such is the case with the JOC, whose profile grew significantly in the post-2000 period. According to a former Cabinet Minister, the JOC, and not Cabinet or the politburo, is the pivotal authority in Zimbabwe:

> JOC is not a statutory or constitutional entity. JOC is the centre of state power in Zimbabwe. It is the system. JOC's pivotal role is particularly pronounced during elections. This is because of the obvious reason that elections are strategically important for deciding who gets into power, or stays in power, or gets out of power, when and how (Moyo 2019).

---

3   'New warning to Mugabe rivals', *CNN*, 9 January 2002.

Table 4: Governance by Police and Militarised Operations

Operation *Sovereign Legitimacy*, 1998	A military operation in the DRC to shore up the Kabila government. Zimbabwe was part of a SADC intervention force.
Operation *Murambatsvina*, 2005	An operation 'to drive out filth' or 'restore order' in urban and rural centres.
Operation *Garikai/Hlalani Kuhle*, 2005	A housing programme set up in the wake of *Murambatsvina*.
Operation *Maguta*, 2005	Organised to oversee increased production of food crops.
Operation *Sunrise*, 2006	Aimed at curbing hyperinflation.
Operation *Chikorokoza Chapera*, 2006	A campaign against small-scale miners and panners.
Operation *Dzikisai Mitengo (Reduce Prices)*, 2007	Aimed at shops and supermarkets to force them to reduce prices.
Operation *Mavoterapapi (how did you cast your vote)*, 2008	A retributive campaign against those who voted for opposition candidates in 2008 election.
Operation *Hakudzokwi (You will not return)*, 2008	A bloody response to small-scale artisanal diamond miners at Chiadzwa.
Command Agriculture, 2016	A military-linked programme to finance commercial farmers who produced maize for delivery to GMB.
Operation *Restore Legacy*, 2017	A military operation in which Robert Mugabe was toppled from office.
Operation *Chikorokoza Ngachipere*, 2020	An operation against the *Mashurugwi*, violent gangs of small-scale miners

Source: various reports

Other institutions have also confirmed the central role of the JOC in political and economic affairs vis-à-vis Cabinet (UNDP 2008). The secretive body was mooted to have planned Operation *Murambatsvina* in 2005, and the revival of Mugabe's political fortunes after his electoral loss in the first round of the 2008 election.

Zimbabwe's party-system is thus complicated, despite the clarity of its Constitution adopted in 2013. The balance of power and checks between various arms of the state are more theoretical than real. The Office of the

President and JOC have accumulated enormous powers, especially in the past 15 years. The power and ambitions of the military have expanded as their presence in the deep state has been consolidated.

Politics and elections in a fragile democracy

Zimbabwe's party system is adversarial. Until 2000 when a vibrant opposition movement emerged under the MDC, Zimbabwe had a dominant party system under ZANU-PF. Since then, there has been a party system dominated by two or three parties. The ruling party has the status of a premier dominant party followed by the main opposition parties, MDC-Alliance and MDC-T. Its pre-eminence is rooted in its powerful role within the party-state system, as we observed. By its proximity to state institutions, it takes advantage of them to strengthen its electoral position.

For more than two decades after independence, Zimbabwe did not have an independent election commission. However, since its establishment in 2004, the Zimbabwe Electoral Commission (ZEC) has often been mired in controversy. There is generally little trust in its operations by opposition parties and civil society organisations. Viewed as being more accommodating to the ruling party, the ZEC has been tainted due to the staffing of its secretariat, most of who are believed to have come from the military and intelligence services. For example, the head of its secretariat in 2020 was a former military officer. Furthermore, its autonomy is compromised by its dependence on the state for the bulk of its funding.

Perhaps the ZEC's lowest point was its handling of the 2008 election, the outcome of which was widely questioned. While progress has been made in building its capacity and professionalism, its credibility in organising the 2018 election process was severely tested. On the part of most opposition parties, there were genuine fears of rigging in the July election. Such fears and mistrust cast a shadow over some notable progress that the ZEC had achieved in the previous two years. First, it succeeded in introducing the biometric voter registration system resulting in 5.4 million people registering for the 2018 election. An estimated 40% of registered voters were below 35 years of age.

Second, consultations between political parties and CSOs during the registration progress strengthened cooperation between these groups. However, the authoritarian environment of Zimbabwean politics continued to cast a dark shadow on the electoral process. The killing of six protesters who demonstrated against a delay in the release of results in August was indicative of this. The ZEC on its own could not transform that environment, an environment that breeds mistrust, fear and polarisation.

In sum, the credibility of Zimbabwean elections since 2000 has been widely questioned. Not only has transparency of the electoral process been low, but intimidation and violence tend to increase during campaigns and post-election disputes. For instance, about 30 people were killed in the 2000 election campaign. More people were killed in the 2002 and 2008 campaigns, some 200 in the latter. During those elections in which violence has not been widespread, as in 2013, there have nevertheless been significant levels of psychological intimidation and fear amongst voters, especially in rural areas.

The Motlanthe Commission (2008) that probed the post-election violence in August 2018 strongly recommended electoral reforms, including the development of information and communications technology, to enhance the transparent and expeditious announcement of results. Opposition parties in particular have viewed delays in the announcement of election results with suspicion and concern. For his part, a former Cabinet minister, Jonathan Moyo, had little doubt that the 2018 election was rigged by the military; it had full control of the electoral machinery to ensure that they directly manipulated the ZEC's administrative and technical processes (Moyo 2019: xvii). The MDC-A candidate, Nelson Chamisa, disputed the election outcome claiming that he won the presidential vote. Zimbabwean politics has been bogged down in that controversy since 2018. With deep levels of mistrust about how the electoral process is managed, democracy in Zimbabwe remains very fragile.

Postscript: COVID-19 pandemic and development

The economic and social impact of COVID-19 will be far-reaching in Zimbabwe. In a country that was already experiencing an economic contraction of 6% in 2019, the pandemic has worsened this during the lockdowns on economic activities between March and September 2020. The pandemic could not have arrived at a worse time. About half of the population was already in dire need of food assistance, and health facilities were overstretched.

Preliminary estimates indicated a decline in mining and agricultural production and exports. Reduced trade would negatively affect growth, revenues and foreign exchange earnings. Sectors such as tourism would witness a decline of about 80% of arrivals in the first half of 2020. Other effects of the pandemic included a decline in remittances from the diaspora, which amounted to about US$1 billion annually. This will adversely affect access to basic social services and food and increase the vulnerability of many households . In particular, the southern and western parts of Zimbabwe that traditionally depend on remittances from South Africa and Botswana will suffer from the decline.

The informal sector experienced a longer lockdown and some sub-sectors like small taxi operators had not yet resumed activities in September. Travel restrictions and the continuing ban on privately owned transport for rural-urban and inter-city routes were compounding the challenges for the informal sector. Furthermore, informal cross-border trade had not yet resumed in September, adversely affecting many small traders dependent on it.

What then is the trajectory of the pandemic and its impact on Zimbabwe's economy and society? It is difficult to predict. The number of cases increased beyond the 8,000 mark in October, with 230 recorded deaths. Although lockdown measures were relaxed in the fourth quarter of the year, development will continue to be adversely affected.

The government response to the pandemic has been impeded by a lack of resources, even though domestic and external donations have not been insignificant. A stimulus of ZWL18 billion for large and small businesses was promised in the second quarter, but whether the government will raise this money and administer it transparently remains to be seen.

Conclusion

This chapter began by reviewing the development process in the first two decades of independence and observed some structural weaknesses. These related to a deficit in development planning capacity and also to an ill thought out switch to neo-liberal structural adjustment. In later decades, the failure to integrate land reform with manufacturing through the maintenance of historical inter-sectoral linkages was a blow to prospects of industrialisation and sustained growth.

Macroeconomic management was affected by the spreading and deepening of corruption and rent-seeking, especially from the 1990s. Central to the governance process was the use of patronage and extractive institutions that benefitted the ruling elite. Political conflicts reflected desperate bids for access to a diminishing national cake. The role of an increasingly militarised state became central in the governance and development processes in a context of a fragile and defective democracy. The fears of insecurity on the part of this state were evident in its disproportionate response to an opposition movement call on 31 July 2020 for anti-corruption protests.

Zimbabwe must climb out of its quagmire. It cannot be business as usual using the old approaches of development and governance methods. Elsewhere we have recommended five related approaches to get out of the developmental and authoritarian trap (Sachikonye, 2020). Zimbabwe should:

- Revisit how it plans and implements development;
- Forge a broad-based developmental coalition;
- Create conditions for a convergence of development and democracy;
- Pursue national dialogue to achieve a durable political settlement; and
- Craft and implement an effective Social Contract.

References

Biti, T. (2015) *Rebuilding Zimbabwe: lessons from a Coalition Government.* Washington, DC: Centre for Global Development.

Bond, P. (1998) *Uneven Development.* Trenton, NJ: Africa World Press.

——— and M. Manyanya (2003) *Zimbabwe's Plunge.* Pietermaritzburg: University of Natal Press; Harare: Weaver Press.

Bracking, S. (2009) 'Political Economies of Corruption beyond Liberalism: An interpretive view of Zimbabwe', *Singapore Journal of Geography*, 30(1), pp. 35-51.

Bratton, M. (2014) *Power Politics in Zimbabwe.* Boulder, CO: Lynne Rienner.

Catholic Commission for Justice and Peace in Zimbabwe (CCJPZ) and Legal Resources Foundation (1997) *Breaking the Silence, Building True Peace: A Report on the Disturbances in Matabeleland and the Midlands, 1980 to 1988.* Harare: CCJPZ and LRF.

Cliffe, L. and C. Stoneman (1989) *Zimbabwe: Politics, Economics and Society.* London: Pinter.

Gibbon, P. (ed.) (1995) *Structural Adjustment and the Working Poor in*

Zimbabwe. Uppsala: Nordic Africa Institute.

Gono, G. (2008) *Zimbabwe's Casino Economy: Extraordinary measures for extraordinary challenges*. Harare: Zimbabwe Publishing House.

Gordon, G. (1984) 'Development Strategy in Zimbabwe: assessment and prospects', in M.G. Schatzberg (ed.) *The Political Economy of Zimbabwe*. New York: Praeger.

Government of Zimbabwe (GoZ) (1981) 'Growth with Equity: an economic policy statement'. Harare: Government Printer.

_____(1982)Transitional National Development Plan   Harare: Government Printer

——— (1991) 'Framework for Economic Reform, 1991-1995'. Harare: Government Printer.

——— (2002) The 2003 National Budget Statement presented to Parliament on 14 November 2002, Harare:Government Printer

——— (2009) 'Short Term Emergency Recovery Programme'. Harare: Government Printer.

——— (2013) 'Zimbabwe Agenda for Sustainable Socio-Economic Transformation (ZimAsset)'. Harare: Government Printer.

——— (2018) 'Transitional Stabilisation Programme (TSP)'. Harare: Government Printer.

Kadhani, X. (1986) 'The Economy: Issues, problems and prospects', in I. Mandaza (ed.) *Zimbabwe: the political economy of transition*. Dakar: Codesria.

Kanyenze, G., T. Kondo, P. Chitambara and J. Martens (2011) *Beyond the Enclave: Towards a Pro-Poor and Inclusive Development Strategy for Zimbabwe*. Harare: Weaver Press.

Kanyenze, G. (2018) 'Economic Crisis, Structural Change and the Devaluation of Labour', in L. Sachikonye, B. Raftopoulos and G. Kanyenze (eds), *Building from the Rubble: The Labour Movement in Zimbabwe since 2000*. Harare: Weaver Press.

Levitsky, S. and L.A. Way (2002) 'The Rise of Competitive Authoritarianism', *Journal of Democracy*, 13(2), pp. 51-66.

Motlanthe Commission (2018) *Report of the Commission of Inquiry into the 1st of August 2018 Post-Election Violence*. Harare: Government Printer.

Moyo, J. (2019) *Exelgate: How Zimbabwe's 2018 election was stolen*. Harare: Sapes Books.

Reserve Bank of Zimbabwe (RBZ) (2005) *Perspectives on the Ills of Corruption*. Harare: RBZ.

Ranger, T. (ed.) (2003) *Historical Dimensions of Democracy and Human Rights in Zimbabwe, Volume 2: Nationalism, Democracy and Human Rights*. Harare: University of Zimbabwe Publications.

Sachikonye, L. (2012) *Zimbabwe's Lost Decade: Politics, Development and Society*. Harare: Weaver Press.

―――― (2017) 'The Protracted Democratic Transition in Zimbabwe', *Taiwan Journal of Democracy*, 13(1), pp. 117-136.

―――― (2020) 'Elusive development, fragile democracy'. Monograph, Harare: IDI.

Simpson, M. and T. Hawkins (2018) *The Primacy of Regime Survival: State Fragility and Economic Destruction in Zimbabwe.* Cham: Palgrave Macmillan.

Stoneman, C. (1988) *Zimbabwe's Prospects* London: Macmillan.

Transparency International Zimbabwe (TIZ) (2014) *Annual State of Corruption Report, 2014*. Harare: TIZ.

UNDP (2008) 'Comprehensive Economic Recovery in Zimbabwe'. Harare: UNDP.

―――― (2020) 'A Preliminary Assessment of the Socio-economic Impact of Coronavirus (COVID-19) on Zimbabwe'. Policy Brief. Harare: UNDP.

Utete Report (2003) 'Report of the Presidential Land Review Committee on the Implementation of the Fast Track Land Reform Programme'. Harare: Government Printer.

World Bank (1995) *Performance Audit Report.* Washington., DC: World Bank.

Zimbabwe Congress of Trade Unions (ZCTU) (1996) *Beyond ESAP*. Harare: ZCTU.

4

Endowed but cursed? Agrarian and mining accumulation in a changing environment

Easther Chigumira and Hazel M. Kwaramba

Introduction

At the turn of the twenty-first century, Zimbabwe's agrarian sector was changed significantly by the Fast Track Land Reform Programme (FTLRP), which resulted in the rapid transformation of land ownership from approximately 6,000 white commercial farmers to mainly black smallholder peasant producers (Moyo 2011; Moyo and Chambati 2013). Coincidentally, in the first decade of land reform declining economic performance in the mineral sector was buoyed by the discovery of surface diamonds (Saunders and Nyamunda 2016; Madimu 2017; Saunders 2018). This was buttressed by progressive policy and legislation toward indigenous economic empowerment for a more inclusive mineral sector.

However, the country's twin drivers of economic activity have done little to propel development. This chapter reviews Zimbabwe's post-independence developmental through the lens of political ecology with focus on the agrarian and mineral economies. It discusses the different cycles of political economy and how these have shaped and impacted the nature-society relationship and in turn the uneven development since independence.

History and context are important for understanding the complex nature of Zimbabwe's land and agrarian question, and the links with the mineral economy. The chapter applies a political ecology approach to understand the effects of the evolving political economy of Zimbabwe on the socio-economic development. It traces the key milestones in the post-independence period and how these impacted the development of the two sectors while also providing 'for (an) understanding the production of nature and how subaltern classes contest the remaking of nature in their struggle to build livelihoods' (Karriem 2009: 318).

The promised land, governance and disillusionment: 1980-1990

The first multi-racial election in 1980 brought into power a black government, officially marking the end of colonial rule in Zimbabwe. The nationalist hopes of a 'nation-state' came to fruition, although fraught with racial imbalances. Colonial capitalism by its very nature had perpetuated uneven development across race, geography and most visibly in the apportionment of land, wherein:

> white 'agrarian bourgeoisie', some 6,000 farmers, retained 39% of the land, some 15.5 million hectares of prime agro-ecological farmland, while one million black households remained confined to 41.4% of the land, 16.4 million hectares of marginal land (Moyo and Yeros 2005: 171).

The post-colonial government's policy priority aimed at achieving social justice, reducing the social and economic gaps between blacks and whites, and meeting the key demand of the government's most populous constituency, the peasantry, through the redistribution of land and a shift in agricultural extension to support black farmers (McCandless 2000; Hanlon et al. 2012).

It is important to note that Zimbabwe acquired independence through the assistance of Eastern Bloc countries, and hence socialist thinking dominated most of its most of its socio-political programmes. The 'willing buyer willing seller' clause in the Lancaster House Constitution was a liberal idea and forced the government to adopt a market-assisted rather than a radical land redistribution programme. Further, this framework, under the guise of a policy of national reconciliation, prevented a radical redistribution of land, and maintained the status quo of white-owned large-scale commercial farming (Palmer 1990). Reconciliation aimed to prevent the exodus of skilled white commercial farmers and preserve the country's food self-sufficiency, since 90% of food supplies came from this group (ibid.). Peasant production had decreased significantly due to out-migration as people escaped the war, and three-quarters of this population had been confined to protected villages (ibid.).

The new government, despite the constraints imposed by the Lancaster House Constitution, embarked immediately on land redistribution under the Land Reform and Resettlement Programme (LRRP) Phase I:

> Resettlement was first carried out under an intensive program of limited scope, using detailed planning ... and providing a wide range of infrastructural and supporting services. Subsequently, parts of the program were implemented using an accelerated approach and expanded quantitative targets (Waeterloos and Rutherford 2004: 538).

According to **Sukume et al.** (2004) these peasant occupations differed from those under the FTLRP in that they took place on uncontested land abandoned by white farmers during the war. Because of the 'willing buyer willing seller' clause, the land offered to the government on the market was mostly in marginal agro-ecological regions III, IV and V and 81% of the resettlement schemes from this phase are located in these drier regions (Masiiwa and Chipungu 2004).

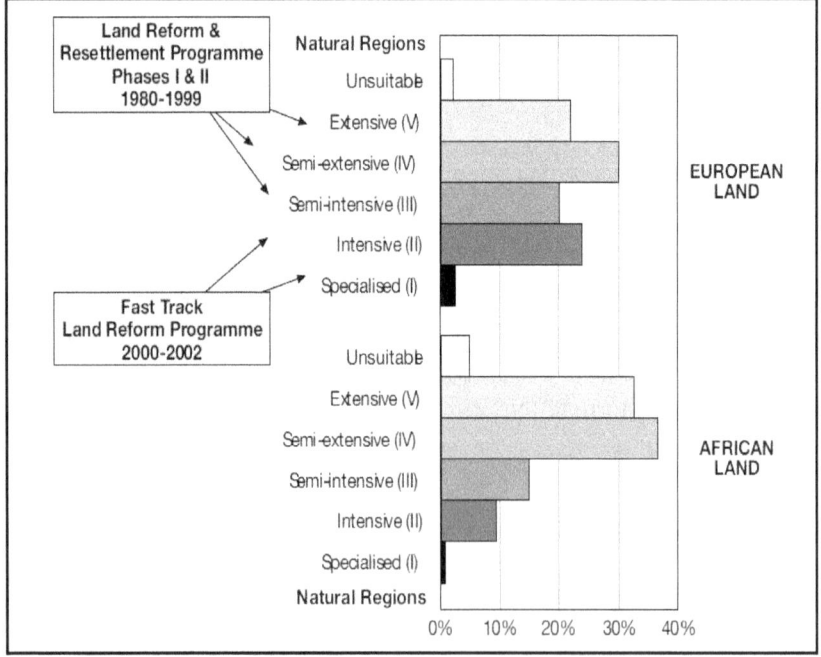

Source: Fox, Chigumira and Rowntree (2007)

In relation to mining, the 1980s continued to be characterised by the dominance of international capital and large-scale mining led by conglomerates such as Rio Tinto and Anglo-America. Gold continued to be the country's main mineral export, due to government support. For example, in 1984 the Reserve Bank of Zimbabwe introduced a gold stabilisation scheme to protect miners against the effects of price volatility. According to Mawowa (2013), although small-scale gold and chrome mining was viewed as important for promoting the entry of black miners, it was not until the 1990s that a significant number of black miners came to the fore.

Waning of post-independence hope: 1990-2000

This decade marked the expiry of the racially biased clauses to the Lancaster House Constitution and enabled the Government to amend these clauses or change the constitution in its entirety. The second decade of independence was characterised by the introduction of the neo-liberal Economic Structural Adjustment Programme, which led to slow redistribution of land, increased cost of living, food riots by the urban population, high rates of unemployment and a drop in real incomes (Marquette 1997; Kanyenze 2004). According to Moyo (2011), Zimbabweans' hunger and demand for arable land was a response to the political consequences of this poor economic environment, rising unemployment and a decline in wages. The war veterans, among others, were disgruntled by the slow pace of land redistribution, and by the fact that government had made no significant progress in narrowing the gap between the colonised and coloniser, except for the upper stratum of the population (Moore 2010).

The significant decline in the macro-economy, which contributed to deindustrialisation, resulted in the movement of labour from the formal to informal sectors in search of alternative livelihoods (Chigumira 2018). Consequently, gold panning and artisanal small-scale mining in mineral-rich regions increased phenomenally and became a refuge from the unemployment problems faced by the country (Shoko and Veiga 2004). The government then introduced new regulations that allowed Rural District Councils to license artisanal miners (Spiegel 2009). In addition, Fidelity Printers, the gold buying agency for the RBZ, allowed for artisanal miners to deliver small quantities of gold and offered higher prices for this (Mawowa 2013). Chigumira (2018) argues that this policy shift aimed to curb civil unrest posed by increased unemployment and economic hardships, because the cyclical linkages of support and cooperation between urban and rural households involving cash remittances had significantly declined.

While government had become supportive of small-scale miners, there was still disaffection by certain sectors of the population with the Lancaster House Constitution, which symbolised the continued dominance of British imperialism and international capital (Sadomba 2008). As a result, several political and civic groups, including the war veterans, began to advocate for a home-grown Constitution, to which government acquiesced. However, the process of re-writing the new Constitution set in motion two sets of bipartisan alliances: on the one hand between the war veterans and government, and on the other between civil society and academics from the country's universities, as well as the white commercial farmers.

In February 2000, the government-sponsored Constitution was put to a referendum and was rejected by the populace. Whites, who in the past two decades since independence had not involved themselves in Zimbabwe's electoral process, took a 'war of position' to protect their landed interests, mobilised their workers to vote against the Constitution and also aligned themselves with civic groups, trade unions and the newly formed Movement for Democratic Change.

3. Transformational change and black economic empowerment: 2000-2020

The argument advanced in this chapter follows the reasoning that nations, communities and individuals may have to reach a certain level of consciousness before they can perceive their space differently and be called to make decisions and participate in government initiatives. This ushers in conscientisation's major strength as a notion of analysis as it brings into focus other important concepts like social identity, power relationships and identity construction, which may be important in shaping a collective mentality critical to the transformation of the new resettled farmers in achieving the goal of black economic empowerment (BEE).

According to Freire (1970: 19), conscientisation is the process of 'learning to perceive social, political, and economic contradictions, developing a critical awareness so that individuals can take action against the oppressive elements of reality'. This approach is an affirmation of Soja's (1985: 90) argument that 'spatiality situates social life in an active arena where purposeful human agency jostles problematically with tangential social determinations to shape everyday activity, particularise social change, and etch into place the course of time and the making of history'. The concept of emancipative beliefs is adopted and placed in the political and social arena in which different stakeholders jostle for equitable space to meet their development, empowerment and conservation needs, and even their hidden political agendas.

Land, minerals and black consciousness

This chapter borrows from the theory of social space to broach the subject of leveraging BEE through the agricultural and mineral economies. The theory of social space is concerned with analyses of the perceptions and relationships within and across various groups, as a way of locating the obstacles to enhancing capabilities (Sen 1984) in the operationalisation of agriculture and small-scale mining. The role of confidence building is integral to the raising of the self-esteem. Brohman (1996) posits that people must first be empowered to determine their own goals, needs, and desires for development. Second, they must be given opportunities to benefit economically and socially. The FTLRP and the Indigenisation and Economic Empowerment Act were important programmes for empowering the subaltern. The argument advanced is that one can only empower individuals who have presented themselves for empowerment. Perhaps the first stage may be to create an environment in which the subaltern feels free and motivated to be part of indigenisation through economic processes and the FTLRP. This would accelerate the creation of a genuine transformative context and space for black consciousness and empowerment.

Following the work of Davidson et al. (2007) on emotional geography, this chapter further posits that the human world is constructed and lived through emotions (Bondi 2005) and that insights into emotional relations or encounters are important in the production of knowledge. Emotional geographies 'attempt to understand emotions – experientially and conceptually – in terms of their socio-spatial mediation and articulation rather than as entirely interiorised subjective mental state. (Davidson et al. 2007: 3). The chapter argues that the FTLRP and the indigenisation policy on the mineral economy (discussed later in the section) can be considered important to 'unshackling the chains of colonialism'. In a way, the large-scale white dominated commercial farming that persisted following independence was a continuing symbol of settler colonialism.

For black Zimbabweans, cultural hegemony was based on the 'colonial legacy' that perpetuated their second-class status. The acquisition of white-owned large-scale commercial farms under the FTLRP signified the final process of decolonisation (Moyo and Yeros 2005). The FTLRP thus reawakened the political consciousness of black Zimbabweans. Frantz

Fanon (2001) argues for violence against the coloniser as a means of unshackling the African from colonial bondage. Hence the symbolism in the use of emotional militaristic discourse and terms such as Chimurenga, that was used during the farm occupations to ensure that the masses knew that the programme embodied the struggle for complete liberation from colonialism. The struggle for emancipation from (neo)colonialism draws parallels with other global rural land occupations movements, ranging from the MST in Brazil, Zapatista in Mexico, FARC in Columbia and UNOKRA in the Philippines to more recent movements in Africa – albeit with varying modes of mobilisation and land occupations – e.g. in South Africa, Malawi and Ghana. While these global movements are diverse in their approaches, ideology, strategy and tactics, they share the same social base, opposition to neo-liberalism and neo-colonialism and are militant on land and agrarian reforms by employing land occupation tactics within the countryside.

Freire (1978) asserts that individuals might experience an epiphany and see themselves in the context of a new reality, but in truth, that reality is constructed to manipulate the individuals. It is envisaged that when the oppressed understand that manipulation and alienation exist, this realisation becomes the stepping-stone to experiencing the process of conscientisation. However, that process in itself does not take place in a vacuum. Berta-Avila (2003) points out that the process can be gradual or accelerated, depending on the conditions created for dialogue and reflection. From the Zimbabwean perspective, authentic becomes the act of naming the reality in which one exists with the understanding that reality is never static. As Berta-Avila (ibid.: 119) states, 'it is a worldview or a historical outlook that puts into perspective the experiences' that in this case black Zimbabweans confront in their daily lives. 'Voice' becomes the political action that challenges the domination that wants to keep the marginalised nameless and voiceless. In this way the FTLRP provided that voice.

This process brought back memories of the past and a subsequent need for blacks to unshackle themselves from other colonial institutions. Chigumira's (2014) study of three resettled communities in Sanyati District showed the movement from traditional catholic and protestant churches (which were largely found in communal and old resettlement areas) to traditional African or syncretic forms of religion such as the *Vapostori* in Fast Track areas. The FTLRP provided a space for people to practice their syncretic religion and commune with the spirit world more openly. The study points out how these syncretic religious beliefs became an important institution in safeguarding the physical environment. Furthermore, land recipients from this study who employed labour preferred to employ married men who could live and work with their families on the farm, which is another example of an African consciousness aimed at reversing colonial experiences, where male laborers had to leave their families in communal areas to work in white areas. Consequently, Chigumira's work shows the redistribution of land through the FTLRP restructured labour relations in a way that ruptured past signifiers of colonialism.

The de-racialisation of commercial farming (Moyo 2013) under the FTLRP changed the unequal racial power relations that had previously existed and therefore represented symbolic progress to settlers. The FTLRP physically and psychologically liberated land recipients from the white man because they had taken back their land and *nhaka* (legacy). As a result, settlers felt they could communicate as equals with whites (Chigumira 2014). The legacy of the FTLRP can be seen through the symbolic representation of the emancipation of the subaltern African wherein prior the African had seen himself as lesser than the white man as signified by lack of ownership or control of land and mineral resources.

Within the mineral economy, Moyo (2011: 502) argues that the land reform programme also opened new avenues for income generation, such as small-scale gold mining, since it entailed the 'liberation of mineral resources, which had been hidden under the monopolistic large scale commercial farms.' Moyo's salient observation was that much more was gained from redistributing land, primarily because it also led to increased access to other natural resources on the same land (Mkodzongi 2013). According to Magure (2012), it was noteworthy that the ruling party's 11th National People's Conference held in Mutare in December 2010 was titled 'Total Control of our Resources through Indigenisation and Empowerment'. At this conference ZANU-PF resolved to accelerate and broaden the indigenisation and empowerment programme. The arrangement was meant to ensure that local employees and managerial staff own and control key productive sectors of the economy, particularly in mining. This would be done through the employee and management share ownership scheme in foreign-owned companies under the auspices of the Indigenisation and Economic Empowerment Act. This Act was touted as a critical milestone to complete the revolution and completely unshackle the country from international capital.

Companies that implemented the share ownership schemes were Schweppes Zimbabwe, which disposed of a 51% stake to employees and management, and Meikles Limited, whose employees received a 20% stake in the company. Similarly, Magure (ibid.) reported that British American Tobacco Zimbabwe had placed a 21% stake with its employees and local groups in compliance with the indigenisation policy. Community share ownership schemes were also structured within mining conglomerates. Section 14B of the Economic Empowerment (General) Regulations of 2010 provided that local communities whose natural resources are being exploited must receive shares in the business entities. Community share ownership schemes countrywide were: the Zvishavane Community Share Trust (Mimosa Platinum Mine); Chegutu-Mhondoro-Ngezi Zvimba Community Share Ownership Trust (Zimplats Mine); and the Tongogara Community Share Ownership Trust (Unki Mine).

Transformation through land reform

Several decades have passed since the implementation of FTLRP. Debates continue to be fraught with emotion and remain highly polarised (Cliffe et al. 2011). The narrative that justifies this programme is based on moral arguments over redressing the past colonial injustices and demand for land by the poor (Mamdani 1996; Moyo and Yeros 2005; Moyo, 2011; Hanlon et al. 2012). From this perspective, the FTLRP is perceived as an historic epoch that is progressive – marking Zimbabwe's true moment of decolonisation – and achieving social justice and BEE. Moyo and Yeros (2005) and Chigumira (2014, 2018) argue that the FTLRP has created the social and economic foundations for a more meaningful democratisation process, and a tri-modal agrarian structure under peasant production at the forefront as the pillar for economic growth and development.

The process of re-peasantisation is about people gaining access to land and entering the 'peasant condition' and 'peasant mode of production' from other backgrounds (van der Ploeg 2008), while quantitatively it entails growth in the number of peasant/smallholder farmers. Re-peasantisation through the FTLRP not only de-racialised the former large-scale commercial farms but also paved way for more ethnically diverse and inclusive territories. The new socially differentiated peasantry comprised of people drawn from differing demographic, socio-economic, regional and ethnic backgrounds, including landless people, unemployed youths, urban workers, entrepreneurs, and former farm-workers and subsistence farmers from communal and old resettlement areas. The new peasantry identified foremost as either an A1 farmer or A2 commercial producer, rather than along regional and ethnic lines.

The effects of Zimbabwe's FTLRP were varied, ranging from a decline in production in the fifteen major agricultural commodities to 'capital strike' in tobacco (Mazwi et al. 2019; Scoones et al. 2017). Initially, with the implementation of the FTLRP, the number of registered tobacco growers plummeted, but then surged after 2003 as A1 farmers ventured into tobacco production (Mazwi et al. 2019). Scoones et al. (2017) herald the tobacco boom led by the smallholder farmers as one of Zimbabwe's post-FTLRP achievements. As a result of the land redistribution, tobacco production provided the foundation of new patterns of asset accumulation by small-scale farmers (Mazwi et al. 2020). Prior to the land reform programme, 1,500 large-scale (predominantly white) tobacco farmers produced 97% of tobacco, but by 2013 the number of indigenous smallholder farmers rose to 110,000, producing around 65% of the crop.

Isolation from the Western bloc following the FTLRP saw the government pursuing a 'Look East Policy,' which Moyo and Nyoni (2013) infer as the catalyst for growth in tobacco contract farming and the significant growth in the number of tobacco growers. The expansion of the contract farming system facilitated the growth of the industry. The government supported a shift to this model as a way to address cost-related barriers faced by smallholder farmers wishing to grow tobacco. By 2017, there were 38,103 A1 tobacco farmers, 7,658 A2 farmers, 46,621 communal farmers and 6,545 small-scale commercial farmers involved in tobacco farming (TIMB 2017). In 2014, one of the highest yields in the post-fast track land reform period was recorded, when over 216 million kg was produced, trading at an average price of US$3.17 (ibid.).

Interestingly, there was also an increase in the number of auction floors. Prior to land reform, there were only two auction floors, Boka Tobacco Auction Floors and Tobacco Sales Floor. With the growth of contract firms changes in tobacco marketing also took place, which facilitated in the boom. Tobacco marketing branched into two systems, namely, auction floors and contract floors. Communal farmers dominated the auction floor markets while contract sales are dominated by A1 and A2 growers (Chambati et al. 2018). Critically, this value chain has become an important model for the transformation of Zimbabwe's agriculture and food system into an US$8.2 billion industry, with which the 'new dispensation' anchors its vision to attain a middle-income status by 2030.

Retrogressive agrarian development

On the other hand, it is important to provide a counter narrative to Zimbabwe 40 years on. This argues that the redistributive programme, which sought to re-peasantise a formerly viable commercial farming sector, has brought an end to modernity and resulted in the abandonment of development (Worby 2003; Richardson, 2005). The argument is advanced through an economic lens, with particular reference to Zimbabwe's macroeconomic plunge during a decade of crisis (Bond and Manyanya 2002) and a focus on production trends since implementation of the programme (Raftopoulous et al. 2003; Selby 2006). From this viewpoint, the FTLRP is regarded as retrogressive and destructive of the agricultural foundations of the country, impinging on food security and turning Zimbabwe from the 'bread-basket' of Southern Africa to a 'basket case' (Wiggens 2004; Richardson 2005; Bond 2007).

Dore (2012) criticises the studies by Scoones et al. (2010) and Hanlon et al. (2012) for their focus on single agro-ecological regions – Mazowe and Masvingo. The argument is that these single case studies cannot be seen as evidence of a successful agrarian reform programme, that only large-scale, intensive and highly specialised holdings can provide sufficient food to meet the needs of the world's population (van der Ploeg 2008) and is therefore the driver for economic growth in rural localities. Notably, this viewpoint ignores the fact that for all the years that the commercial farms were in place, the rural economy did not grow inclusively with blacks as stakeholders, rather they were labourers living in substandard accommodation with limited access to education and virtually no prospects outside the farms.

For countries undertaking land and agrarian reform programmes, the debate over land distribution (large versus small-holder agriculture) is seen as a struggle between Chayanovian and Leninist positions. Essentially, Lenin wanted the confiscation of large estates and nationalisation of land, whereas Chayanov argued for all land to be transferred to peasant farms (van der Ploeg 2014). Zimbabwe adopted the Special Maize Programme for Import Substitution (Command Agriculture) Scheme in 2016 to promote access to financing for the smallholder sector. Command

Agriculture initiatives entailed government's guarantee/security to a private company to supply inputs to farmers and also incentives to farmers to deliver their produce to the Grain Marketing Board. Chisango (2018) postulated that instead of being a panacea to food security problems bedevilling communities, the programme faced numerous challenges that included corruption in the allocation of resources, increased public expenditure, non-repayment of loans, and continued low productivity among smallholder farmers, most of whom were practicing dryland farming and were susceptible to climate-related shocks. Government availed financing as shown in Table 1 below.

This implies very high and increasing non-payment rates in addition to a net cost to the government of about 1.9% of GDP in 2017 and 0.7% in 2018 (World Bank 2019). The challenges of the Command Agriculture system necessitated a shift to Commercial Smart Agriculture in 2019, which is now run under the Commercial Bank of Zimbabwe, with government as a guarantor.

Table 1: Government Command Agriculture Expenditure

Year	Finance Availed USD	Recovered USD	Non-payment Rates
2016	105,000 000.00	-	-
2017	439,000 000.00	47, 000 000.00	54%
2018	238,000 000.00	81, 300 000.00	81%

Source: World Bank (2019)

When viewing cereal production over the last 20 years by the new A1 and A2 farmers vis-a-vis production prior to 2000, it is evident as shown in Table 2 below that production levels are low. Current maize grain production is 24% below the 5 year average of 1.2 million MT. Yield by communal farmers remains very low at 0.33 MT/hectare in comparison to the 1.82 by A2 (medium-large scale) farmers. The A2 farmers are still producing below their expected potential. Government's smart commercial agriculture programme (formerly Command Agriculture) expects A2 farmers to produce at least 5 tonnes of maize per ha. (GoZ 2020).

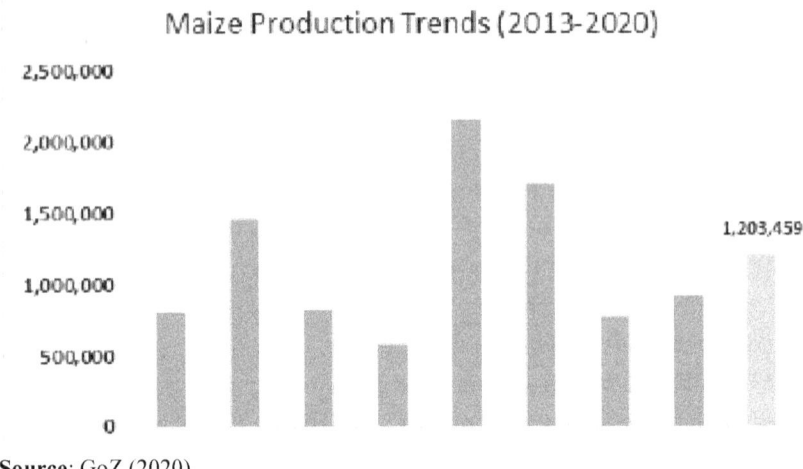

Source: GoZ (2020)

In view of the aforementioned declining production trends, the current argument is that Zimbabwe has reversed its agrarian development gains through the FTLRP. It has failed to follow the historical experiences of the Asian tigers – Japan, South Korea, Taiwan, Vietnam and China – where redistribution of land to smallholders and subsequent agricultural growth stimulated industrialisation and urbanisation (Griffen et al. 2002). Instead, land distribution to smallholders has not generated higher rates of economic growth through a multiplier effect to other parts of the economy, compared to land concentrated in the hands of a relatively few individuals (as in large-scale farming) as posited by Jayne et al. (2003). Poverty levels are considerably higher and solely practicing agriculture has not provided secure livelihoods for peasant households.

Blessing or curse? The windfalls of mineral resources

Madimu (2017) offers insights on farmer-miner-State contestation, which he describes as constituting a 'long and entangled relationship', which was informed by the laws set by the British South African Company, which favoured mining at the expense of farming (Madimu 2017). Kusena (2015) and Kufakurinani and Bhamu (2015) take a food security based approach in highlighting the impact of resource-based conflicts in Zimbabwe and the intricate linkages between conflicts and food (in)security in Zimbabwe. Kusena (ibid.) argues that the establishment of diamond mining companies in Chiadzwa in 2006 altered the livelihoods of the host communities especially when they were resettled. As a result, the Marange diamonds are perceived as a curse rather than a blessing due to constraints in the beneficiation chain (Kusena 2019).

The discovery Marange's alluvial diamonds accentuated and deepened existing fault lines in state-society engagements around resources, and exposed the frailty of resource governance strategies in situations characterised by weak governance and institutional capacity, powerful executive authority and polarised political environments (Saunders 2018). 'Diamondisation' was a failed opportunity for the country to harness its natural resources and build back better after years of recession and hyperinflation from the purported annual US$2 billion dollar industry. Elite capture and rent-seeking behavior turned the resource into a curse marred by contestation, corruption and violence (Saunders 2018). The then Minister of Finance, Patrick Chinamasa acknowledged the management failure of Marange, observing that, 'there was greater economic impact from diamonds during times of uncontrolled alluvial panning than what is being realised following introduction of formal diamond mining arrangements' (Chinamasa 2016).

Mlambo (2016) considers citizens to be victims of the participation by local small-scale and semi-large-scale operators in the extractive industry. NGOs take an intergenerational justice approach in emphasising the significance of economic, environmental and social rights. Central to this approach are concerns for the environment and the individual/collective rights of the community. NGOs have called for the reformation and transparency of the country's mining sector (Mtisi 2016), and their narratives implicate the State in threatening environmental, economic and social rights in the sector.

The influence of the State spearheads elite accumulation and patronage through politicising the extraction and trading of natural resources (Mawowa 2013). Unfortunately, this has resulted in local communities being the losers. As an example, the diamond industry failed to improve indicators of development – electricity, access to safe and portable water, sanitation, etc. – for the local communities in Marange and the surrounding districts of Buhera, Chipinge and Chimanimani. Forty years on, international capital and a handful of elites linked to it are the winners of Zimbabwe's natural resource endowment, while the majority remain cursed and bound by the chains of poverty.

Reconfiguring the agriculture and mining sector for the future

The chapter recognises the role played by the FTLRP and the indigenisation and empowerment policies set by the government to reverse the division of land by race, and in physically and psychologically emancipating black Zimbabweans from the 'shackles of colonialism'. Chigumira (2018) argues that the Fast Track widened the peasant-base in the country through an increase in the number of smallholders by consolidating and creating new peasant household units under the A1 and A2 small-scale resettlement.

This chapter concludes that land reform can transform the lives of poor peasants by removing distortions in the land ownership structure which allows them access to land and other natural resources which are critical for their social reproduction strategies and livelihoods security. The Fast Track opened up the rural landscape for a broad base of people from diverse backgrounds that straddle different social classes from both rural and urban areas. It provided for greater integration of rural and urban spaces, with resettled areas offering opportunities for short-term wage employment for unemployed urbanites and urban spaces providing alternative commodity markets for resettled farmers (Chigumira 2018). However, women and young people are still at the margins of this broad-based development despite progressive legislation that ensures their title to land. The progressive quotas set for their access to land have not been met and women continue to be on the margins of financial inclusion.

The peasant economy is an intrinsic feature of Zimbabwe 40 years on, countering the development theory that sees a linear pathway to modernity and development through a transition from a peasant-based to a highly industrialised society with large-scale farming as the anchor. The politics of patronage and elite capture have been key to the windfalls of the mineral economy – the curse of the resource described by Kaulemu and Sachikonye in Chapters 2 and 3. The mineral economy has failed to stimulate real developmental growth and poverty rates continue to increase. Through land reform, the new farmers gained unique opportunities, and ASM has also become a key livelihood activity, especially during the dry season when people are not farming. Notably, the country has not successfully harnessed its potential to grow and develop the rural economy despite its rich endowments.

The failure to harness Zimbabwe's natural resources in a way that benefits the majority can also be attributed to what Kamete (2007, 2012) calls the 'pathologisation of informality' due to continued use of exclusionary colonial legislation such as the Regional Town and Country Planning Act of 1976. The Act, premised on British planning law, articulates formality, order and a healthy and aesthetically pleasing environment as the norm for rural and urban development. This 'pathologisation of informality' in the mineral economy and other sectors of the economy have in fact made the state less responsive to the changing socio-economic environment characterised by high unemployment, deindustrialisation and increased levels of informality.

Failure to understand that development is not linear, and that informality is another pathway for the attainment of livelihood and economic goals, is incongruent with the current realities in the country. Forty years after independence, and with the majority of economically active people being in the informal sector, revisiting the normative perception of development and policy support is imperative in order to allow the realisation of desired developmental outcomes for the majority.

Conclusion and recommendations: Where do we go from here?

The intention of this chapter was not to merely write about history and its injustices, rather to take account of the past and assess how it impacts on the success of present development policies. Zimbabweans have experienced progress on inclusion and natural resource management to some extent, although by no means adequately so. A progressive development approach should be designed and implemented to enhance capacities to promote self-leadership and ownership of the development process. It is important to enforce institutional arrangements that allow the agriculture and small-scale mining sectors to bear the costs, thus promoting responsibility and entrepreneurial steering. Additionally, it will foster greater cooperation, organisation and collaboration among sector players and with businesses and networks for advanced value chain development.

Entrepreneurial economic development goals have to be communicated, understood and recognised by citizenry, and not only by the government and the business sector, as is seemingly the case now. Undeniably, this may appear to be a more cumbersome and less appealing approach, but without a detailed intervention the goal of attaining development in Zimbabwe will remain elusive.

Hanlon et al. (2012) argue that Rhodesian and post-independence governments gave much support to white farmers and therefore the Fast Track farmers require the same level of support in order to thrive. Kinsey's long-term study of old resettlement areas shows a strong correlation between state support and farmer productivity (Kinsey, 1999). Mabeza-Chimedza (1998) talks of the miracle revolution among communal farmers in the 1980s and attributes it to state support through extension services and subsidies. While the government attempted to support farmers with input subsidy schemes this has come at a cost to the fiscus. As such, it is recommended that government creates an enabling business environment for agriculture through (a) policies and regulations that are consistent; (b) research and development; (c) strong and improved extension support and farmer training; and (d) public-private partnerships to fund and subsidise agriculture to support the new farmers.

Rukuni's (2013) suggestions continue to be relevant today: (i) Short-term financing for inputs and working capital; (ii) medium term (2-5 years) finance for machinery, irrigation and infrastructure development; and (iii) long-term finance (6-25 years) for building large infrastructure such as dams.

Furthermore, on the agrarian front, a holistic land policy needs to be put in place which charts the future for agriculture in Zimbabwe across the tri-modal agrarian structure that has been created since the FTLRP. There needs to be clarity of tenure for both A1 and A2 farmers. Present tenure arrangements of offer letters, confirmation letters and *jekes* (cards with plot numbers of the occupant of land) are not tradeable. The proposed 99-year lease as a legal document is not tradeable until all title deeds are remitted, and leases are registered. Creating a comprehensive cadastre and land administration and governance system can bring about this clarity. Increased tenure security based on an updated cadastre will provide incentives for farmers to make long-term investments in their farms and is likely to motivate an increase in production and productivity. An updated cadastre will also provide an important basis for establishing a National Spatial Data Infrastructure (NSDI), which currently does not exist. NSDI is an effective mechanism for generating, organising, coordinating, sharing, exchanging and leveraging geospatial information for decision-making and a location-based platform of action.

Despite the Indigenisation and Empowerment Act, large-scale mining remains in the hands of international capital, while the ASM is the driver for local capital accumulation and poverty alleviation. As such, there needs to be recognition that 40 years on, ASM, like Fast Track smallholder farming is integral to Zimbabwe's modern development trajectory and therefore an enabling policy and business environment needs to be created. Existing mining laws and policies, which focus on the 'established' small-scale mining entrepreneurs, need to better appreciate that ASM is still, for many, a vital source of income (Mkodzongi and Spiegel, 2018). This implies formal recognition of ASM without the need for registration of the miners given the itinerant nature of the *makorokoza*, and supporting the ASM value chain and technologies.

References

Berta Avila, M. (2003) 'The Process of Conscientization: Xicanas/Xicanos Experiences in Claiming Authentic Voice', *Journal of Hispanic Higher Education,* 2(2), pp. 117-128.

Bond, P. and M. Manyanya (2002) *Zimbabwe's Plunge: Exhausted Nationalism, Neoliberalism and the Search for Social Justice*. Harare: Weaver Press.

Bond, P. (2007) 'Zimbabwe in Crisis: Local, National, and Regional Perspectives', *Safundi: The Journal of South African and American Studies*, 8(2), pp. 149-181.

Bondi, L. (2005) 'Making connections and thinking through emotions: between geography and psychotherapy,' *Transactions of the Institute of British Geographers*, 30(4), pp. 433-448.

Brohman, J. (1996) 'New directions in tourism for third world development', *Annals of Tourism Research*, 23(1), pp. 48–70.

Chambati, W., F. Mazwi and S. Mberi (2018) 'Contract Farming and Peasant Livelihoods: The Case of Sugar Outgrower Schemes in Manhica District, Mozambique'. Harare: SMAIAS.

Chigumira, E. (2014) 'Re-peasantization under Fast Track Land Reform: Implications for Livelihood and Landscape Change, Sanyati District, Zimbabwe'. PhD thesis, University of Oregon.

Chigumira, E. (2018) 'Political ecology of agrarian transformation: The nexus of mining and agriculture in Sanyati District, Zimbabwe,' *Journal of Rural Studies*, 61, pp. 275-276.

Chinamasa, P.A. (2016) 'Zimbabwe: the 2016 National Budget Statement: "Building a Conducive Environment that attracts Foreign Direct Investment"'. Presentation to the Parliament of Zimbabwe by the Minister of Finance and Economic Development on 26 November, 2015.

Chisango, F.F.T. (2018) 'Challenges and Prospects of Zimbabwe's Command Farming in Unlocking the Country's Smallholder Agricultural Economy', *International Journal of Agricultural Economics*, 3(4), pp. 76-82.

Cliffe, L., J. Alexander, B. Cousins and R. Gaidzanwa (2011) 'An Overview of Fast Track Land Reform in Zimbabwe: Editorial Introduction', *Journal of Peasant Studies*, 38(5), pp. 907-938.

Davidson, J., L. Bondi and M. Smith (eds) (2007) *Emotional Geographies*. New York: Routledge.

Dore, D. (2012) 'Myths, Reality and The Inconvenient Truth about Zimbabwe's Land Resettlement Programme'. Discussion Paper. Harare: Commercial Farmers Union of Zimbabwe.

Fanon, F. (2001) *The Wretched of the Earth*. London: Penguin.

Fox, R.C., E. Chigumira and K.M. Rowntree (2007) 'On the Fast Track to Land Degradation? A case of the impact of the Fast Track Land Reform Programme in Kadoma District, Zimbabwe', *Geography*, 92(3), pp. 212-224.

Freire, P. (1970) *Pedagogy of the Oppressed*. New York: Herter and Herter.

——— (1978) *Pedagogy in Process: The Letters to Guinea Bissau*. New York: Continuum.

Government of Zimbabwe (GoZ) (2020) 'Second round crop and livestock assessment report, 2020'. Harare: Ministry of Lands, Agriculture, Water and Rural Settlement.

Griffen, K., A.R. Khan and A. Ickowitz (2002) 'Distribution of Land and Poverty,' *Journal of Agrarian Change*, 2 (3), pp. 279-330.

Hanlon, J., J. Manjengwa and T. Smart (2012) *Zimbabwe Takes Back its Land*. West Hartford, CT: Kumarian Press.

Jayne, T.S., T. Yamano, M.T. Weber, D. Tschirley, R. Benfica, A. Chapoto and B. Zulu (2003) 'Smallholder income and land distribution in

Africa: implications for poverty reduction strategies', *Food Policy*, 28, pp. 253-275.

Kamete, A.Y. (2007) 'Cold-hearted, negligent and spineless? Planning, planners and the rejection of filth in urban Zimbabwe', *International Planning Studies*, 12(2), pp. 153–171.

———— (2012) 'Interrogating planning is power in an African city: Time for reorientation?' *Planning Theory*, 11, pp. 66–88.

Kanyenze, G. (2004) 'The Zimbabwe economy 1980-2003: a ZCTU perspective', in D. Harold-Barry (ed.), *Zimbabwe: The Past is the Future. Rethinking Land, State and Nation in the Context of Crisis*. Harare: Weaver Press.

Karriem, A. (2009) 'The rise and transformation of the Brazilian landless movement into a counter-hegemonic political actor: A Gramscian analysis,' *Geoforum*, 40, pp. 316-325.

Kinsey, B. (1999) 'Land reform, growth and equity: emerging evidence from Zimbabwe's Resettlement programme', *Journal of Southern African Studies*, 25(2) pp. 173-196

Kufakurinani, U. and W. Bhamu (2015) '"Resettled and Yet Unsettled?" Land Conflicts and Food (in)security in Insiza North, Zimbabwe, 2005-2013', in Z. Makwavarara, R. Magosvongwe, and O. Mlambo, *Dialoguing Land and Indigenisation in Zimbabwe and Other Developing Countries*. Harare: University of Zimbabwe Publications.

Kusena, B. (2015) 'Coping With New Challenges: The Case of Food Shortage Affecting Displaced Villagers Following Diamond Mining Activity at Chiadzwa, Zimbabwe, 2006-2013,' *Journal of Sustainable Development in Africa*, 17(2), pp. 14-24.

———— (2019) 'Rural Food Security in Mutare District, Zimbabwe, 1947-2010'. PhD thesis, Rhodes University, South Africa.

Mabeza-Chimedza, R. (1998) 'Zimbabwe's smallholder agriculture miracle', *Food Policy*, 23(6), pp. 529-537.

Madimu, T. (2017) 'Farmers, Miners and the State in Colonial Zimbabwe (Southern Rhodesia), c.1895-1961'. PhD thesis, Stellenbosch University, South Africa.

Magure, B. (2012) 'Foreign investment, black economic empowerment and militarised patronage politics in Zimbabwe', *Journal of Contemporary*

African Studies, 30(1), pp. 67–82.

Mamdani, M. (1996) *Citizen and Subject: Contemporary Africa and the Legacy of late Colonialism*. Princeton, NJ: Princeton University Press.

Marquette, C. (1997) 'Current Poverty, Structural Adjustment and Drought in Zimbabwe', *World Development*, 27(7), pp. 1141-1149.

Masiiwa, M. and L. Chipungu (2004) 'Land Reform Programme in Zimbabwe: Disparity Between Policy Design and Implementation', in M. Masiiwa (ed.) *Post-independence land reform in Zimbabwe: controversies and impact on the economy*. Harare: Friedrich-Ebert Stiftung and Institute of Development Studies, University of Zimbabwe.

Mawowa, S. (2013) 'The Political Economy of Artisanal and Small-Scale Gold Mining in Central Zimbabwe', *Journal of Southern African Studies*, 39(4), pp. 921-936.

Mazwi, F., A. Chemura, G.T. Mudimu and W. Chambati (2019) 'Political Economy of Command Agriculture in Zimbabwe: A State-led Contract Farming Model', *Agrarian South: Journal of Political Economy: A triannual Journal of Agrarian South Network and CARES*, 8(1-2), pp. 232-257.

Mazwi, F., W. Chambati and G. Mudimu (2020) 'Tobacco contract farming in Zimbabwe: power dynamics, accumulation trajectories, land use patterns and livelihoods', *Journal of Contemporary African Studies*, 38(1), pp. 1-17

McCandless, E. (2000) 'Reconciling Relationships while pursuing justice: The case of land redistribution in Zimbabwe', *Peace and Change*, 25(2), pp. 225-238.

Mkodzongi, G. (2013) 'New People, New Land and New Livelihoods: A Micro-study of Zimbabwe's Fast-track land Reform', *Agrarian South Journal of Political Economy*, 2(3), pp. 345-366.

―――― and S. Spiegel (2018) 'Artisanal gold mining and farming: Livelihood linkages and labour dynamics after land reforms in Zimbabwe', *Journal of Development Studies*, 55(10), pp. 2145-2161.

Mlambo, A.S. (2016) '"Zimbabwe is not South African province": Historicising South Africa's Zimbabwe policy since the 1960s', *Historia*, 61(1), pp. 18-40.

Moore, D. (2010) 'A decade of disquieting diplomacy: South Africa,

Zimbabwe and the ideology of national democratic revolution, 1999-2009', *History Compass*, 8(8), pp. 752-767.

Moyo, S. (2004) *The Land and Agrarian Question in Zimbabwe*. Harare: SAPES Books.

—— (2004) 'Farm Sizes, Decongestion and Land Use: Implications of the Fast-Track Land Redistribution Programme in Zimbabwe'. *AIAS Monograph Series*, 2.

—— (2011) 'Land Concentration and accumulation after redistributive reform in post-settler Zimbabwe,' *Review of African Political Economy*, 38(128), pp. 257-276.

—— (2013) 'Land reform and redistribution in Zimbabwe since 1980', in S. Moyo and W. Chambati (eds) *Land and Agrarian Reform in Zimbabwe: Beyond White Settler Capitalism*. Dakar: Codesria.

—— and W. Chambati (eds) (2013) *Land and Agrarian Reform in Zimbabwe: Beyond White-Settler Capitalism*. Dakar: Codesria.

—— and N. Nyoni (2013) 'Changing agrarian relations after redistributive land reform in Zimbabwe', in S. Moyo and W. Chambati (eds), *Land and Agrarian Reform in Zimbabwe: Beyond-White Settler Capitalism*. Dakar: Codesria.

—— and P. Yeros (2005) 'The Resurgence of Rural Movements under Neo-liberalism,' in S. Moyo and P. Yeros (eds), *Reclaiming the Land: The Resurgence of Rural Movements in Africa, Asia and Latin America*. London: Zed Books.

—— and P. Yeros (2013) 'Crisis and Global Transformation: What role for Re-peasantization?', *Agrarian South: Journal of Political Economy*, 2(3), pp. 241-245.

Mtisi, S., M. Dhliwayo and G. Makore (2011) 'Extractive Industries Policy and Legal Handbook: Analysis of the key issues in Zimbabwe's mining sector – case study of the plight of Marange and Mutoko mining communities'. Harare: Zimbabwe Environmental Law Association.

Mtisi, S. (2016) 'Enforcer or enabler? Rethinking the Kimberley Process in the shadow of Marange', in R. Saunders and T. Nyamunda (eds) *Facets of Power: Politics, Profits and People in the Making of Zimbabwe's Blood Diamonds*. Harare: Weaver Press.

Murisa, T. (2018) 'Land, Populism and Rural Politics in Zimbabwe'. Paper presented at the Emancipatory Rural Politics Initiative (ERPI), Conference Paper No.51, International Institute of Social Studies, The Hague.

Palmer, R.H. (1990) 'Land Reform in Zimbabwe, 1980 – 1990', *African Affairs*, 89(355), pp. 163-181.

Raftopoulos, B., A. Hammar and S. Jensen (eds) (2003). *Zimbabwe's Unfinished Business: Rethinking Land, State and Nation in the Context of Crisis*. Harare: Weaver Press.

Richardson, C.J. (2005) 'The Loss of property rights and the collapse of Zimbabwe', *CATO Journal*, 25(2).

Rukuni, M. (2013) 'Broadening and deepening rural financial services and land banking'. Bulawayo: Sokwanele.

Sadomba, W. (2008) 'War Veterans in Zimbabwe: Complexities of a liberation movement in an African post-colonial settler society'. PhD thesis, Wageningen University.

Saunders, R. (2018) 'High-Value Minerals and Resource Bargaining in a Time of Crisis: A Case Study on the Diamond Fields of Marange, Zimbabwe.' Working Paper 2018-1. Geneva: United Nations Research Institute for Social Development.

——— T. Nyamunda (eds) (2016) *Facets of Power: Politics, Profits and People in the Making of Zimbabwe's Blood Diamonds*. Harare: Weaver Press.

Scoones, I., N. Marongwe, B. Mavedzenge, J. Mahenehene, F. Murimbarimba and C. Sukume (2010) *Zimbabwe's Land Reform, Myths & Realities*. Woodbridge: James Currey.

Scoones, I., B. Mavedzenge, F. Murimbarimba and C. Sukume (2017) 'Tobacco, contract farming, and agrarian change in Zimbabwe', *Journal of Agrarian Change*, 18(1), pp. 22-42.

Selby, A. (2006) 'Commercial farmers and the State: interest group politics and land reform in Zimbabwe'. PhD thesis, University of Oxford.

Sen, A.K. (1984) *Resources, Values and Development*. Oxford: Basil Blackwell.

Shoko, D. and M. Veiga (2004) 'Information about project sites in Zimbabwe'. Global Mercury Project report.

Soja, E.W. (1985) 'The Spatiality of Social Life: Towards a Transformative Retheorisation', in D. Gregory and J. Urry (eds), *Social Relations and*

Spatial Structures. London: Macmillan.

Spiegel, S. (2009) 'Resource policies and small-scale gold mining in Zimbabwe'. *Resource Policy*, 34(1-2), pp. 39-44.

Sukume, C., S. Moyo, and P. B. Matondi (2004) 'Farm Sizes, Decongestion and Land Use: Implications of the Fast-Track Land Redistribution Programme in Zimbabwe'. AIAS Monograph.

Tobacco Industry and Marketing Board (TIMB) (2017) 'Annual Statistical Report'. Harare: TIMB.

van der Ploeg, J.D. (2014) 'Peasant-driven agricultural growth and food sovereignty', *The Journal of Peasant Studies*, 41(6), pp. 999-1030.

——— (2008) 'The third agrarian crisis and the re-emergence of processes of repeasantization', *Rivista Di Economia Agraria*, LXII (3).

Waeterloos, E. and B. Rutherford (2004) 'Land Reform in Zimbabwe: Challenges and Opportunities for Poverty Reduction among Commercial Farm Workers', *World Development*, 32(3), 537-553.

Wiggens, S. (2004) 'Food security options in Zimbabwe: multiple threats, multiple opportunities?' London: Overseas Development Institute.

Worby, E. (2003) 'The End of Modernity in Zimbabwe? Passages from Development to Sovereignty', in A. Hammar, B. Raftopoulos and S. Jensen (eds), *Zimbabwe's Unfinished Business: Rethinking Land, State and Nation in the Context of Crisis*. Harare: Weaver Press.

World Bank (2019) *Zimbabwe Public Expenditure Review with a Focus on Agriculture*. Washington, DC: World Bank.

5

Development Aid and the Politics of Development

George Mapope

Introduction

The 18th of April 2020 marked 40 years of Zimbabwe's political independence after 90 years of colonisation. Soon after independence, the new government embarked on a programme of reconstruction and development with the support of bilateral and multilateral donors. In general terms, the process of reconstruction was fairly successful as the economy was re-capitalised and reintegrated into the world economy (Sichone 2003).

The prevalence of embedded structural inequalities along racial lines and a dual economy meant that the government had to institute political structures that would break the duality and shift the balance of power from minority institutions to majority ones. The process of delivering economic and social justice was premised on breaking a dual economy that was entrenched in nine decades of white minority rule (Kanyenze et al. 2011). With alternating epochs of hope, dystopia and indifference, Zimbabwe's path to development has confounded expectations.

The role of aid in the development process has received considerably less attention and analysis. Various hypotheses can be postulated based on empirical experiences. At one end of the continuum, Dambisa Moyo's (2009) key arguments strongly advocate against issuing foreign aid to development countries on the pretext that it takes away citizen agency from their governments, festers corruption and makes the poor worse off. Other scholars and political leaders have similarly viewed aid as an instrument of foreign policy to influence local political and development processes. At the other end, aid is viewed in a positive light as essential for catalysing development through good governance, humanitarian assistance and social protection.

In Zimbabwe, the dynamics of aid and the politics of development vary from one epoch to another. The first decade of independence from 1980 to 1990 is touted as a golden era of development in which the state, aided by international development assistance, achieved modest development outcomes. The second decade was one of adjustment, in which the state was forced to retreat to pave way for greater private sector participation. However, this was accompanied by deteriorating social development outcomes under a structural adjustment programme. The third, in which the state morphed into a 'radical authoritarian' state, witnessed significant economic decline and a changed landscape for development assistance. It saw considerable reduction in official aid with the country mainly receiving aid for enhancing good governance, and for institutional strengthening and humanitarian emergencies.

Various questions deserve attention. How much aid has the country received over time and how has it shaped development processes and outcomes? What has been the nature of relations between the state and donors in different epochs and what explains the changing dynamics and implications? What role can development aid potentially play in the future of the country's development process? In addressing these questions, the chapter also considers the role that future aid could play in influencing development outcomes in Zimbabwe.

The anatomy of development aid

There is general agreement in literature that development aid is a legacy of the aftermath of the Second World War. The then United States Secretary for State, George Marshall, crafted an audacious plan to bail out European economies after a ravaging war. The aid package, which was in excess of US$50 billion, would double up to assist in the reconstruction of the continent and act as a countermeasure against the spread of communism (Berger and Beeson 1998). The overwhelming success of the Marshal Plan in channeling resources from the United States to a war-torn Europe convinced many western leaders that a similar transfer of resources to newly independent countries in Asia and Africa would likewise lead to rapid development and poverty alleviation.

In general, development aid involves a voluntary transfer of cash or in-kind resources from governments or financial institutions in more economically advanced countries to needy countries with the goal of improving the human conditions in the receiving countries (Ajayi 2000; Lancaster 2007). Such aid can be bilateral, multilateral or private and is usually offered according to need and the discretion of the donor.

A close examination of both democratic and authoritarian donors reveals that they have political, economic, geostrategic or self-interested motives, with development in the recipient country being a secondary objective. The primary objectives of aid for donor states are to catalyse trade, enhance access to extractive resources and political influence rather than to facilitate economic and social development of the recipient countries. Since its origin in the form of the Marshall Plan, aid has been used as a foreign policy tool. The idea of aid was novel in such a formal and institutional form because there was no precedent of such financial incentives between states to win each other's alliance and allegiance through the exercise of soft power (Nye 2018).

Development aid and growth

Historically speaking, the idea of altruism has been part of the practice of international co-operation, particularly during periods of crises, whether man-made political conflicts or natural calamities and disasters. However, the link between development aid and economic growth is not obvious. Big push theorists argue that extending aid in large quantities will certainly lead to income creation and demand enhancement which in turn enlarges the market and leads to industrialisation (Rosenstein-Rodan 1943). The connection between security and growth from the 1950s to the present day provides a common thread from which to gain a deeper understanding of the varied reasons for help. The Marshall Plan was not only aimed at rebuilding Europe but also at preventing communism from spreading on the continent (Hinds and Windt 1991). In 1951, the United States adopted the Mutual Security Act, which made explicit the link between military and economic aid programmes and the technical assistance provided to 'underdeveloped' countries. Indeed, development aid in the sense of defence considerations and expanding spheres of influence dominated the discourse up until the end of the Cold War (Alesina and Dollar 2000).

Martens (2001) argues that loans restrict the effectiveness of development aid because recipients have to repay them in the medium- or long-term. Even if the rate of interest and repayment conditions are well below market levels, these funds are only temporary aid. Zimbabwe's external loan debt has averaged US$8 billion, or 53% of GDP, since 2000, dating back to the structural adjustment years. While the initial loan may have been put to some good use, the debt that emanates from interest payments stifles domestic resource mobilisation.

It must also be noted that large aid inflows do not necessarily result in general welfare gains, and the high expectation of aid may increase rent-seeking and reduce the expected public good. Moreover, there is little evidence to suggest that donors take corruption seriously into account while providing aid (Svensson 1998). A permanent rise in foreign aid reduces long-run labour supply and capital accumulation. Furthermore, it increases long-run consumption and has no impact on long-run foreign borrowing. Contrary to this, supporters of aid such as Joseph Stiglitz (2003), Jeffrey Sachs (2005) and Roger Riddell (2007) counter these arguments, charging that aid has brought more good than harm. They cite countries that have received substantial aid with successful track records such as Botswana, South Korea and Indonesia. The aid conditionality is not sufficient and the penalties are not hard enough when recipient countries deviate from their commitments. In fact, Riddell (2007) claims that there are incentives for aid donating agencies to disburse as much aid as possible.

> **Box 1: The Korean experience with development aid**
>
> Korean economic growth in the post-war period is partially due to well-managed development assistance. According to Korean government estimates, the country received US$12.7 billion between 1945 and the late 1990s, 'which helped spur economic development and decrease poverty' (OECD, 2008: 9). The use of aid in South Korea was a product of negotiation between the donor (who in this case was dominantly the US) and the recipient Korean government.
>
> During the reign of General Park between 1961 and the time of his assassination in 1979, South Korea positioned itself well in the fast lane to development with impressive growth rates. This is because the new government's approach to development assistance changed drastically with all foreign loans invested to support diverse sectors of South Korea's economy, including agriculture and fishing, manufacturing, and infrastructure.

There are a number of examples where development aid has led to massive poverty reduction, improved social services and competent public institutions; notable examples are South Korea, Botswana and Honduras. The Korean experience shows that development can indeed be achieved through bilateral and multilateral aid flows that are properly planned and managed.

Closer home in Southern Africa, Botswana is one of the success stories, where aid contributed towards broad-based socio-economic development. At Botswana's independence in 1966, it was one of the poorest countries in the world, and dependent on UK grants for all of its development funding and much of its recurrent expenditure (Maipose et al. 1996). It maintained one of the fastest economic growth rates in the world in the decades that followed, and is now a middle-income country with a GDP per capita of more than US$7,000.

Botswana adopted centralised aid management, which has several positive consequences: it ensures that donor projects coincide with government priorities, it allows for full accounting for counterpart and recurrent costs, and it facilitates donor coordination. Part of the success of development aid in Botswana, therefore, came from the high commitment to ownership of aid that other transformers like South Korea had in abundance. The result was that aid coupled to other sources of revenue, such as diamonds, put Botswana in the fast lane to development.

Criticisms of development aid

While aid has been shown to contribute to long-term growth in a number of countries, there has been growing criticism of it. From the outset, development assistance has incited animated debates about the underlying reasons why rich countries provide assistance to poor countries. Scholars and politicians question the altruistic and selfless gestures aimed at improving the well-being of recipient populations. Three schools of thought – the neo-liberal, the radical leftists and the populist realists – have inspired criticism of development aid. In recent days, the aid system's most vociferous critics seem to include an improbable fusion of these.

The neo-liberal criticism emphasises the perverse effects of aid on growth and development through swelling of the staff of ineffective public administrations, backing corrupt and non-democratic leaders, stifling entrepreneurialism and inducing dependency among the recipients (Bauer 1971; Easterly 2006). Dambisa Moyo (2009) bemoans the granting of over US$1 trillion dollars of aid money over the last 60 years with little to show for it, and exhorts Africa to take charge of its own destiny and adopt market-friendly policies.

The increase in Chinese aid inflows to Zimbabwe through the Look East Policy, for example, can be analysed from this perspective. China has been at the forefront of exerting power through its doctrine of 'non-interference' with the affairs of the recipient countries. In both the Mugabe and the post-Mugabe eras, China has been painted as Zimbabwe's all-weather friend through its aid and lending policy. The strategic approach of the Chinese has been to extend grants and loans to governments that have fallen out of favour with western financiers without giving them any conditions on transparency or governance reforms. Zimbabwe has indeed received beneficial loans and grants, but some have been under opaque circumstances; examples include funds for the construction of the new parliament building at Mt Hampden and the Zimbabwe Defence University with the latter costing about US$100 million.

China has obtained concessions for strategic mining projects in platinum, diamonds, gold and chrome. Beyond Chinese aid, the policy has also seen the both the Mugabe and the Mnangagwa governments closely associating themselves with other emerging economies such as India, the Russian Federation and Belarus. The creation of the policy also meant that the debt strategy had to be aligned with it; during the GNU era, traditional debt relief methods were considered to be conceding defeat to the West, and thus unacceptable (Biti 2014).

Development aid and growth in Zimbabwe

Siavhundu (2020) tested the link between foreign aid and economic growth in Zimbabwe using ordinary least squares methodology for longitudinal data spanning 1991 to 2016. He found that foreign aid negatively influenced Zimbabwe's economic growth with a 10% increase in ODA leading to economic contraction by a factor of 2.2%. He concluded, however, that aid on its own does not present barriers to economic growth; problems may relate to issues such as the quality of the institutions that are expected to complement the effectiveness of aid. Foreign aid granted to the Zimbabwean government certainly made tremendous contributions to the economy but the stipulations that accompanied it compromised its purpose. Regardless, Zimbabwe's development as measured by the Human Development Index (HDI) continued to plummet from a high of 0.5 in 1990 to an all-time low of 0.425 in 2005. Thus, despite the development aid that was channelled into health and education, overall human development remained depressed due to declining levels of income between 1995 and 2005, and the HIV/AIDS pandemic .

Moyo and Mafuso (2017) concluded that although Zimbabwe received substantial foreign aid up to 2000, empirical data shows that this has not been effective. It was also evident that although Zimbabwe enjoyed considerable growth in the 1980s, it experienced a sudden decline in the 1990s (Sachikonye, 2012). Social indicators show that the economy was collapsing at the same time as foreign aid inflows stopped coming in.

Zimbabwe's three aid epochs and the attendant development outcomes

Several bilateral and multilateral agencies have extended development aid to Zimbabwe since its independence, including the World Bank, the IMF, and the AfDB as the key multilateral players, and the US, the UK, China and Scandinavia. Over the past three decades, USAID has focused on strengthening Zimbabwe's health systems, improving standards of living, supporting democratic processes, and enabling economic growth. Early USAID contributions providing loans for home construction for over 40,000 low-income households, investing over US$170 million in factories and farms to increase the productivity of industry and smallholder farmers, supporting community-based natural resource and wildlife management, and funding thousands of Zimbabweans to attend university in the United States.

Figure 1: Trend in multilateral aid flows into Zimbabwe

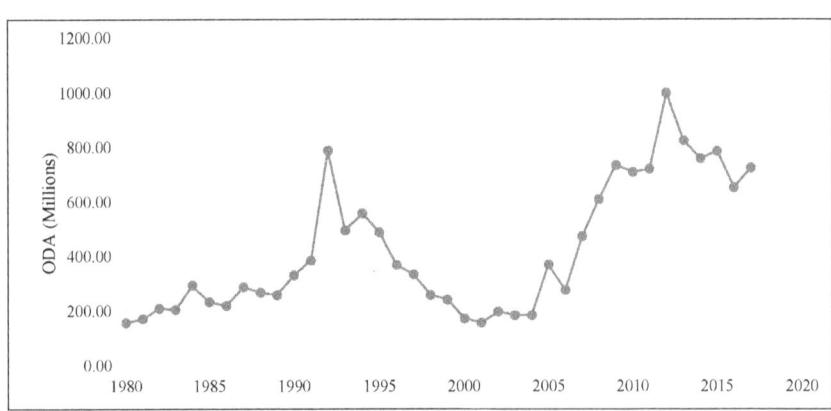

Source: Constructed from World Bank Data

As in many countries across Africa, there was an alarming spread of HIV/AIDS in Zimbabwe in the 1990s. USAID has coordinated with the Government of Zimbabwe and international donors to provide HIV/AIDS antiretroviral drugs and prevention services to reduce the national HIV infection rate from 26% at its peak to 14%. Figure 1 shows the trend of flows of multilateral aid in Zimbabwe.

The first aid and development epoch: 1980 to 1990

The first epoch saw the new state's development priorities buoyed by the windfall of support from donors, which coincided with the UN 'decade of development in the global south'. The hostility of the cold war was gathering momentum and western democracies were keen to see the transformation of former socialist party governments.

Table 1: ODA to Zimbabwe from the IMF, World Bank and AfDB, 1980-1990 (US$).

Year	IMF	World Bank	AfDB
1980	0.00	0.00	0.00
1981	0.00	104,917,535.80	0.00
1982	0.00	45,478,573.51	25,342,914.53
1983	0.00	133,760,761.05	57,229,136.30
1984	2,058,441.00	36,467,117.09	0.00
1985	0.00	9,668,219.07	67,798,983.37
1986	0.00	10,000,000.00	0.00
1987	0.00	0.00	0.00
1988	0.00	130,121,817.97	28,612,977.32
1989	0.00	0.00	19 286 995.95
1990	0.00	127,243,010.98	145,017,034.56
Total	2,058,441.00**	597,657,035.50	343,288,042.00

Source: Constructed from World Bank Data

Within two years of independence, Zimbabwe was a recipient of at least 14 World Bank loans and four IDA credits totalling US$657 million for reconstruction and development (Dashwood, 2000). Of those loans, at least US$51 million was channelled to the development of the agricultural sector, particularly in the communal areas US$136 million went to the rehabilitation and expansion of the manufacturing sector with a focus on export oriented businesses; US$150 million was channelled towards expansion of energy generation, and US$141 million was dedicated to the development of the transport sector.

While the 1980s could be viewed as a decade of relative prosperity, particularly when measured by social indicator changes, the drawback was the high cost of unsustainably large budget deficits. Although not high on a global scale, Zimbabwe's growth rate of 4.3% per annum during the eighties was higher than that of sub-Saharan Africa as a whole.

The second aid epoch and structural adjustment years: 1991 to 2000

From 1991, the government of Zimbabwe implemented the Economic and Structural Adjustment Programme (ESAP), whose key element according to Kanyenze (2004) was a radical shift from an import substitution oriented economy to an open-market system anchored on export-led growth and monetary policy reform. The result was an avalanche of development aid mainly from multilateral institutions, the IMF, the World Bank and the AfDB as shown in Table 2.

Table 2: Multilateral aid inflows to Zimbabwe, 1991-2000 (US$)

Year	IMF	World Bank	AfDB
1991	0.00	62,386,243.86	15,218,604.29
1992	216,150,000.00	299,810,150.15	180,428,222.49
1993	65,656,168.00	226,592,641.86	31,966,823.47
1994	76,642,125.00	0.00	11,090,644.20
1995	75,492,900.00	0.00	1,686,232.22
1996	0.00	32,990,742.50	0.00
1997	0.00	4,037,287.79	1,940,910.99
1998	53,802,392.00	5,796,928.56	39,074.27
1999	32,233,993.00	88,856,697.27	0.00
2000	0.00	0.00	0.00
Total	519,977,578.00	720,470,691.99	242,370,511.93

Source: Compiled from World Bank Data

Over the years, the government incurred persistent budget deficits, which were used primarily to support recurrent expenditure rather than investments in infrastructure or productive assets. As a result, the debt burden increased significantly. Up to 1994, Zimbabwe's total debt was less than 60% of GDP, but from 1995 it rose sharply, reaching 90% of GDP in 2000 (Makina 2010).

Nevertheless, failure to productively invest development aid, especially during 1990-2000, resulted in the further weakening of the Zimbabwe dollar, with the exchange rate falling sharply from Z$8.45 to the US dollar in 1995 to over Z$100 by 2000. Moreover, this slump was accompanied by a decline in the human development index from 0.5 in 1990 to 0.45 in 2000. By the end of the second aid epoch, the economy was in free fall, fuelled by Zimbabwe's participation in the DRC war and the unbudgeted war veterans' compensation scheme. Regardless of the quantum of financial resources that donor agencies pumped into the country, the underlying fiscal policy environment and expenditure patterns guaranteed the failure of any development interventions.

Development aid in an era of radical authoritarianism

The third and final aid epoch is the ongoing era, post-2000. The country's land reform programme in 2000 triggered sanctions against Zimbabwe to which the ZANU-PF government responded with a radical form of authoritarianism to retain power. The sanctions, imposed by multilateral financial institutions, the United States and the European Union, meant that Zimbabwe was ineligible to access financial and technical assistance, and saw voting rights and balance of payments support suspended.

In the era of radical authoritarianism, widespread corruption and the institution of sanctions meant that the issuance of foreign aid was transformed from direct budget support into humanitarian aid, activities that support democracy, governance and the rule of law. As a result, the relationship between most aid agencies and the government has been very volatile, with agencies criticised for meddling in local politics and being drivers of the regime change agenda (Gukurume 2012). The World Bank's development assistance to Zimbabwe totalled $1.6 billion between 1980 and 2000, after which the Bank suspended direct lending due to non-payment of arrears. In 2002, the government briefly suspended the operations of a number of relief agencies; since then, relations between the international aid community and the government have been characterised by mistrust (Bird and Busse 2007).

Zimbabwe's development assistance is rife with a lack of accountability rendering it highly fungible by corrupt politicians who use it for their own primary purposes, such as obtaining political capital at the cost of national development purposes. Thus, well-intentioned aid sometimes contributes to weakening the opposition forces and strengthening ZANU-PF.

Perceptions of foreign aid in Zimbabwe, as in many other African countries, have been shrouded in ambiguity. Some view foreign aid as the universal panacea to a plethora of challenges, while others portray foreign aid as part of the problems. To this end, many people, particularly ZANU-PF politicians, have scoffed at foreign aid. Although they accept it, they view the operations of NGOs with suspicion and this saw the government repealing the Private Voluntary Organisations (PVO) Bill and replacing it with the NGO Bill. The impact of the new Bill was to significantly increase the power of government granted under the original legislation (International Bar Association 2004).

Development assistance appears to establish and entrench patronage and donor-to-recipient client relationships. International aid flows to Zimbabwe have also plummeted considerably following the breakdown of ties between Harare and the western capitals. ZANU-PF has blamed donor agencies for using their economic muscle to support regime change, thus the relationship between ZANU-PF and foreign donor agencies has been characterised by constant tension and controversy (Gukurume 2012).

The period between 2009 and 2013 signifies a post-2000 island in the relations between Zimbabwe and the donor community due to the gains made by the inclusive government. The government of national unity (GNU) formed between ZANU-PF and the two MDC formations instituted reforms which included the removal of regressive policies centred on export surrender requirements, unjustifiable protectionism, market interference through price controls and a more positive attitude towards wealth creation (Biti 2014). While many of such reforms and social protection programmes were later slowed by the ZANU-PF government, they were not entirely reversed. The post-GNU government halted the expansion of the Harmonized Social Cash Transfer (HSCT) programme and donors continued to assist existing beneficiaries. Continuing dependence on humanitarian aid shows that the politics of development is also a product of Zimbabwe's engagement with the international community.

Some academics have argued that aid tends to foster dependency. Ironically, the Zimbabwean government even defaulted on foreign debt payments and reached the point that in order to clear the external debt, it would be competing for resources that could have been devoted to productive investment in health and social sectors. The steady deterioration of the economy since ESAP led to widening budget deficits (Moyo and Mafuso 2017).

In October 2000, the World Bank suspended lending to Zimbabwe due to the country's financial mismanagement and non-service of its debt obligations. Similarly, after its annual Article IV consultation in mid-September 2001, the IMF called on Zimbabwe to clear its debts before financial aid could resume. In 2001, the US Senate adopted the Zimbabwe Democracy and Economic Recovery Act (ZIDERA), which determined the US and EU foreign policy toward Zimbabwe and toward Southern nations that were sympathetic to Zimbabwe (ibid.). Zimbabwe was subjected to economic sanctions as a collective penalty on the ruling party for its poor human rights record and irreversible but controversial land reform programme.

Debt per capita averaged US$670 between 1980 and 2001. It is possible that borrowed development assistance contributed to the improvement of the economy and better social services for the majority of the population, but this was negligible, and the debt kept ballooning. In 1980, the ratio of external debt to GNP was 12.5%, but in 2000 it rose to 56%. At this time, aid was coming from China, India, Japan, Indonesia, Iran, South Africa and even Botswana, but it could not ameliorate the crippling debt burden that saw the nation moving steeply into socioeconomic decline and hyperinflation.

While relations between Harare and the US and the EU remained sour after 2000, Zimbabwe has been a recipient of humanitarian assistance and other grants meant to address issues of human rights, climate change and good governance. Programmes like the HSCT have significantly reduced extreme poverty, and the fight against HIV and AIDS was largely funded by the Global Fund and USAID.

The year 2020 saw the global spread COVID-19. The disease was quickly declared a pandemic by the World Health Organisation (WHO) and led to entire cities and countries being locked down with minimal movement for essential services. The immediate impact on local and the global economy is undoubtedly huge and Zimbabwe's economy is predicted to slow down by over 20%. The effects of the pandemic will obviously be more pronounced in the medium term but in the short term, aid agencies have re-directed funds towards mitigating the impacts of the pandemic.

The politics of development in Zimbabwe

Leftwich (1994) claims that if politics consists of all the activities of cooperation, negotiation and conflict in decisions about the use, production and distribution of resources, then the politics of development is about changing not only how resources are used, produced and distributed, but also about how decisions are taken about such changes and about the politics which sustain, implement and extend them.

Zimbabwe, for reasons of ever-changing internal policies, started off as a high-aid high-growth recipient in the first decade of independence, but retreated into the low-aid low-growth stage with the onset of radical authoritarianism, especially after 2000.

Mugabe's 1980 pledge to 'beat swords into ploughshares, so we can attend to the problems of developing our economy' not only failed to materialise by the end of the second decade of independence but de-investment in social services in favour of military expenditure meant that existing ploughshares were being converted into swords. The shift in internal politics as the state apparatus became more repressive, coupled with increasing international isolation, saw the country recede into dystopia. Shumba (2016) conceptualises Zimbabwe as a 'predatory state', in which there is party and military dominance in the state; state-business relations shaped by domination and capture; and state-society relations shaped by violence and patronage.

While the rapid post-2000 socio-economic deterioration had little to do with the withdrawal of development aid, experiences with aid in war-ravaged Europe and South Korea, Honduras and Botswana in more recent years provide glimmers of hope for the country. For Zimbabwe to return to the path of growth with direct budgetary support, the rules of the political game and agreement about the rules are fundamental. These rules are normally expressed in formal institutional agreements, which regulate fair competition. To better understand how politics shape the development process, the concept of development itself needs to be discussed.

The conception of development

The understanding of development has changed considerably from the time when the role of the state was conceived of as ensuring correct policies to stimulate growth, to the rise of neo-liberal development thinking in the 1980s and 1990s. Classical development economists widely held that a large injection of capital generated through savings or international aid was necessary to achieve economic growth. However, the modern understanding of development has transcended economic growth to embrace economic transformation, democratisation and the expansion of human freedoms and capabilities. The conceptualisation of development has shifted to include both the principal means – participation by the state and various non-state actors – and the outcomes.

The conception of development has changed considerably from the classical thinking, when it was equated with economic growth. For classical thinkers, development was limited to the outcomes, which were defined by macroeconomic metrics such as the balance of payments (BOP), gross domestic product (GDP) and gross national product (GNP). The rise of neo-liberal development thinking in the late twentieth century however, pitched development beyond economic growth to include broader structural transformation, democratisation and the expansion of human freedoms and capabilities (Rodney 1972; Sen 1999; Stiglitz 2003). Development has thus shifted to include both the principal means and outcomes. This chapter conceptualises development as a transformative change process involving economic transformation, social progress and political transition into more democratic forms.

As the epistemological conceptualisation of development has shifted, so has the role of the state. In the twentieth century, the idea of the state as an agent of development came to be part of the official policy of western colonial powers in the interwar years (Leftwich 1994). Development does not happen of its own accord due to entrenched structural rigidities; it requires intentional effort under the right political conditions to attain and sustain improvement in human welfare (Wylde 2017). In classical development thinking, the role of the state was conceived of as ensuring an enabling environment through mediating the economic contest between labour and capital to stimulate growth.

An analysis of the behaviour of the Zimbabwean state, especially from 2000, reveals that the it behaved like a Weberian actor which after facing political pressure from opposition MDC party, actively pursued its own survival goals and that of the ZANU-PF party. The state in its current format is unlikely to be capable of underwriting large structural and economic changes with substantive welfare gains even with the support of development aid from multilateral institutions.

The notion that the state has much more than a minimal supervisory role has been central to development theory and practice (Leftwich 1994). Thus, instead of a total rollback of the state in economic development, the relevant question concerns the appropriate nature and scale of state intervention desirable for economic development. Two main views emerge: a facilitative role, and a direct interventionist role. Given the assumed efficient functioning of the market mechanism, government intervention in the economy is viewed as inefficient. This chapter, however, argues that a direct interventionist state that takes ownership of development aid is needed to achieve large-scale improvements in the welfare of its people. As the country moves further along the structural transformation continuum, both the state and the aid mechanism can slowly withdraw and pave way for self-regulating market mechanisms underpinned by local and foreign investment.

Along with state interventionism comes the debate on state capacity to administer aid and deliver development. State capacity includes not just the technical and bureaucratic capacity, but also the political acumen to entice citizens and donors to buy into its development agendas for sustained periods of time, including the nature of state-society relations. Zimbabwe's development programmes have not inspired hope among the country's restless citizens, especially the urban population and the largely unemployed youths. State capacity is not only defined as the characteristics of the state's machinery of delivery, but also by how the machinery is related to the social structures that can influence the nature and pace of development (Evans 1995).

Nevertheless, the capacity of the Zimbabwean state to reward innovation and competitiveness is largely dwarfed by a coterie of historical and ongoing complexities. Rather than wealth creation through production and new services, Zimbabwe's economy is hinged on income generation through redistributive mechanisms based on political connections for the elite and through trading on the margins for the majority of the citizenry. The process of structural transformation cannot take place without a social contract between those who govern, the donors and those who are governed, and it has been elusive due to contestations over electoral outcomes since the MDC entered on the political fray in 2000.

While the government needs resources to carry out its primary functions such as preserving territorial integrity and maintaining its monopoly of legitimate violence, at the very least, and beyond that providing a legal system, public safety and other public goods, such resources must be raised in taxes from the governed. Often, the quantum of taxes collected depends on the goodwill of the taxpayers, particularly for a dominantly informal economy like Zimbabwe's in which the majority of businesses are not fiscalised. The difficulty of raising taxes from such an informal sector places constraints on the government's ability to provide social and economic goods, and to some extent protects the rational self-interests of taxpayers.

During the early stages of development, states foster coordination, facilitate interdependent investment decisions in orchestrated networks of producers and suppliers, establish public development banks and other institutions for long-term industrial finance, and nudge firms to upgrade their technology and move into sectors that fit with a national vision of development goals (Bardhan 2016). On the other hand, Leftwich (2006) asserts that for the state to execute its functions, it must have the capacity to act as

> a central coordinating intelligence or coordinating capacity which can steer, push, cajole, persuade, entice, coordinate and at times instruct the wide range of economic agents and their groupings to go this way instead of that, to do this and not that.

The theory of the Big Push model of development which is credited to Rosenstein-Rodan (1943) was originally used as the justification for foreign aid. This theory hypothesises that increased aid and investments in developing countries mediated by a capable state can kick-start savings and investment, promote growth and reduce poverty.

The key challenge for countries pursuing catch-up development is to create and maintain a minimum institutional architecture that protects private property, enforces contracts and rewards innovation (Tabellini 2004). Leftwich (1994) argues that an effective public capacity for promoting development is not a function of good governance, as currently understood, but of the kind of politics and state that alone can generate, sustain and protect. Since 2000, the Zimbabwean state has been accused of generating and perpetuating the politics of patronage based on an insatiable desire to retain power at all costs. Many aid agencies and multilateral finance institutions have called on Zimbabwe to reform by embracing democratic values as enshrined in the constitution and follow the rule of law to open new lines of credit. The response to such calls has been lukewarm, with former Information and Publicity Minister Professor Jonathan Mojo categorically stating 'ZANU-PF cannot reform itself out of power'.[1]

Towards a trajectory of developmentalism in Zimbabwe

This chapter takes the position that evidence on the contribution of development aid to Zimbabwe's economic development has not been conclusive. Zimbabwe has witnessed epochs of good and dismal economic performance for many reasons that are not linked to the patterns of development aid. Aid may, however, play a crucial role in the reconstruction of the socio-economic landscape of the country. It has also been argued that state capacity is a prerequisite for development to occur regardless of the amount of aid the country receives. It has also been averred that in its current form, the capacity of the Zimbabwean state to manage development aid and lead the country's structural transformation is seriously compromised by both internal and external factors. The existing mix of political and economic institutions is dominantly extractive and is not capable of producing broad-based development in their current form regardless of who is in power.

The political requirement for broad-based development to oversee a process of structural transformation is not only a set of agreed, consistent and coherent institutional rules, but rules which both encourage and allow a politics of development to be mooted and sustained in the medium term. The trajectory towards a culture of developmentalism with rapid structural transformation will thus only take off if the country addresses the structural limitations in its political system. These include, but are not limited to, a government that receives and maintains widespread buy-in in the medium term and reforms in the technical capacity of state institutions to be independent from excessive political interference and increase efficiency in their delivery of political and economic goods.

As it stands, the ever-increasing hostility between ZANU-PF party and the MDC-Alliance means that the country can hardly attract significant investment from outside, or even from within. Moreover, the hostilities mean that the country can hardly get significant development aid that is

---

1 'Zanu-PF will never reform itself out of power, Prof Moyo declares', *Chronicle*, 6 September 2016.

channelled into the productive sectors and also into interventions to help reform the institution of governance. Only after resolving such hostilities can development aid significantly contribute to economic growth and social progress.

References

Ajayi, K. (2000) *International Administration and Economic Relations in a Changing World*. Ilorin: Majab Publishers.

Alesina, A. and D. Dollar (2000) 'Who gives Foreign Aid to Whom and Why?' *Journal of Economic Growth,* 5(1), pp. 33-63.

Balci, A. and M. Yesiltas (2005) 'Using foreign aid as a foreign policy tool: The case of Japan', *Journal of Asian Development,* 2, pp. 167-198.

Bardhan, P. (2016) 'State and Development: The Need for a Reappraisal of the Current Literature', *Journal of Economic Literature*, 54(3), pp. 862-892.

Bauer, P.T. (1971) *Dissent on Development: Studies and debates in development economics.* London: Weidenfeld and Nicolson.

Berger, M.T. and M. Beeson (1998) 'Lineages of liberalism and miracles of modernisation: The World Bank, the East Asian trajectory and the international development debate', *Third World Quarterly*, 19(3), pp. 487-504.

Bird, K. and S. Busse (2007) 'Re-thinking aid policy in response to Zimbabwe's protracted crisis'. Discussion Paper. London: ODI.

Biti, T. (2014) 'Rebuilding Zimbabwe: Lessons from a Coalition Government'. Washington, DC: Centre for Global Development.

Dashwood, H.S. (2000) *Zimbabwe: The Political Economy of Transformation*. Toronto and London: University of Toronto Press.

Easterly, W. (2006) *The White Man's Burden: Why the West's efforts to aid the rest have done so much ill and so little good.* New York: Penguin Press.

Evans, P. (1995) *Embedded autonomy: States and industrial transformation.* Princeton, NJ: Princeton University Press.

Gukurume, S. (2012) 'Interrogating foreign aid and the sustainable development conundrum in African countries: A Zimbabwean experience of debt trap and service delivery', *International Journal of*

Politics and Good Governance, 3(3.4), pp. 1-20.

Hinds, L.B. and T.O. Windt (1991) *The Cold War as Rhetoric: The Beginnings, 1945-1950*. New York, Praeger.

International Bar Association (2004) 'An analysis of the Zimbabwean Non-Governmental Organisations Bill, 2004'. London: International Bar Association.

Kanyenze, G. (2004) 'Economic Structural Adjustment Programme (ESAP): Precursor to the fast track resettlement?' in M. Masiiwa (ed.) *Post-independence land reform in Zimbabwe: controversies and impact on the economy*. Harare: Friedrich-Ebert Stiftung and Institute of Development Studies, University of Zimbabwe.

———, T. Kondo, P. Chitambara and J. Martens (2011) *Beyond the Enclave: Towards a Pro-Poor and Inclusive Development Strategy for Zimbabwe*. Harare: Weaver Press

Lancaster, C. (2007) *Foreign Aid: Diplomacy, Development, Domestic Policies*. Chicago: University of Chicago Press.

Leftwich, A. (1994) 'Governance, State and the Politics of Development', *Development and Change*, 25(2), pp. 363-386.

Leftwich, A. (2006) 'From Drivers of Change to the Politics of Development: Refining the Analytical Framework to understand the politics of the places where we work'. University of York.

Maipose, G.S., G.M. Somolekae and T.A. Johnston (1996) *Aid Effectiveness in Botswana: Botswana's' Management of External Assistance and Case Studies of the U.S./Botswana Bilateral Aid Relationship*. Washington, DC: Overseas Development Council.

Makina, D. (2010) 'Historical Perspective on Zimbabwe's Economic Performance: A Tale of Five Lost Decades', *Journal of Developing Societies*, 26(1), pp. 99-123.

Martens, J. (2001) 'Rethinking ODA: Towards a renewal of Official Development Assistance'. A discussion paper for the United Nations Financing for Development Process. Bonn: World Economy, Ecology and Development Association.

Moyo, D. (2009) *Dead Aid: Why aid is not working and how there is a better way for Africa*. New York: Farrar, Straus and Giroux.

Moyo, L. and L.T. Mafuso (2017) 'The Effectiveness of Foreign Aid on

Economic Development in Developing Countries: A Case of Zimbabwe (1980-2000)', *Journal of Social Sciences,* 52(3), pp. 173-187.

Nye, J.S. (2018) 'China's Soft and Sharp Power'. Prague: Project Syndicate,

Riddell, R. (2007) *Does Foreign Aid Really Work?* Oxford: Oxford University Press.

Rodney, W. (1972) *How Europe underdeveloped Africa.* London: Bogle-L'Ouverture Publications.

Rosenstein-Rodan, P. (1943) 'Problems of Industrialisation of Eastern and South-Eastern Europe', *The Economic Journal*, 53(1), pp. 202-211.

Sachikonye, L. (2012) *Zimbabwe's Lost Decade: Politics, Development and Society.* Harare: Weaver Press.

Sachs, J.D. (2005) *The End of Poverty: Economic Possibilities of our Time.* New York: Penguin.

Sen, A. (1999) *Development as Freedom.* Oxford: Oxford University Press.

Shumba, J.M. (2016) 'Zimbabwe's Predatory State: Party, Military and Business Complex'. DPhil thesis, University of the Witwatersrand.

Siavhundu, T. (2020) Foreign Aid – Economic Growth Nexus: An Empirical Study of the Zimbabwean Case', *PM World Journal,* 9(4).

Sichone, P. (2003) *Zimbabwe: The Political Economy of Transformation.* Toronto and London: University of Toronto Press.

Stiglitz, J.E. (2003) 'Development policies in a world of globalization'. Paper presented at the seminar, New International Trends for Economic Development, Rio de Janeiro, September 12-13.

Svensson, J. (1998). *Foreign Aid and Rent-Seeking.* World Bank Policy Research Paper.

Tabellini, G. (2004) 'The role of the state in economic development'. Working Paper No. 1256. Munich: CESifo.

Wylde, C. (2017) *Emerging Markets and the State: Developmentalism in the 21st Century.* London: Macmillan.

6

Migration and Economic Development in Zimbabwe

Alouis Chilunjika and Medicine Masiiwa

Introduction

Zimbabwe is a community of migrants; people have come from Malawi, the Democratic Republic of Congo, Rwanda, Ethiopia, Mozambique, Tanzania and Zambia. Some thronged the then Rhodesia to work in farms and mines as migrant labourers; others came as refugees. In the past two decades the country has lost a significant number of skilled and semi-skilled workers who migrated to the United Kingdom, the USA, Canada, Australia, South Africa and Botswana in search of greener pastures.

Most people emigrated when the political and economic crisis started and deepened during the 2000-2004. In 2000-2008, more than 2 million Zimbabweans migrated to South Africa, most as economic refugees, as the country fell into a deep economic crisis, with inflation shooting up to 231 million per cent.[1] Zimbabweans who migrated abroad for economic reasons continue to support their family members back home, and contribute to economic growth and development through the return of skills, remittances and investments.

However, the diaspora community is concerned about the poor access to investment and trade related information. Legal frameworks were formulated to make it easier for lower skilled people to seek work abroad

---

[1] 'Renewed exodus of Zimbabweans amid economic woes', *The Zimbabwe Daily*, 27 October 2019.

and offer them social protection, while at the same time strengthening mechanisms for harnessing remittances for economic development. The migration of experienced professionals in health and education sectors has far reaching effects. Migration is increasingly becoming a major human development issue, which, if effectively managed, could contribute towards socio-economic development in Zimbabwe. This chapter explores the impact of migration on Zimbabwe's economic development.

Migration defined

Migration is the movement of people from one place to another with the intention of settling permanently or temporarily. In most cases, the movement is over long distances and from one country to another, but internal migration is also prevalent. There are three types of migration: internal, regional and international. Much of the interest in internal migration in developing countries has focused upon population movements from rural to urban areas (Chikanda and Dodson 2015).

Regional migration is within a country from one county or province to another. International migration entails the movement of people from one country to another. Masiiwa and Doroh (2011) defined international migration as the act of leaving one's country of birth for a foreign country, for various reasons such as seeking a better life, joining families abroad or escaping political prosecution at home. For a long time, migration has been used as a way for households to search for work, improve their livelihoods and increase their incomes, as well as to escape situations of persecution, conflict and poverty (Dagdemir et al. 2018). According to the World Bank (2016), approximately 3.4% of the world population lives in a country other than their country of birth.

The Zimbabwean context

Emigration from Zimbabwe is not a new phenomenon; the migration of Zimbabweans to South Africa to seek job opportunities in the mining industry started as early as the beginning of the twentieth century (Zanamwe and Devillard 2010). Zimbabwe has two migration histories, generally corresponding to the pre-and post-independence periods. This chapter focuses on the latter.

Historically, Zimbabwe has been a country of origin, transit and destination all at the same time (ibid.). Two major phases can be distinguished. The first corresponds to the years immediately following the country's independence in 1980. According to Tevera and Crush (2010), between 1980 and 1984, 50-60,000 whites left the country because they could not adapt to the changed political environment. The second phase, from the 1990s to 2009, shows much more diverse migration patterns (Zanamwe and Devillard 2010). The post-2009 period has seen people migrating predominantly to South Africa.

The socio-politico-economic crisis in Zimbabwe

The dynamics of economic decline during the 1990s shaped economic and political developments in the post-2000 period. The new millennium witnessed an unforeseen socio-politico-economic crisis, which witnessed dwindling employment, hyperinflation, shortages of commodities, rising child mortality rates, falling life expectancy and a governance crisis that included political violence, uncertainty and cultural and social isolationism.

The 2000s were a period of unprecedented political and economic turmoil (Mawowa and Matongo 2010). Unemployment rose to over 70%, resulting in many people leaving the country in search of better opportunities. The national elections of 2002, 2005 and 2008 saw ZANU-PF party members targetting the opposition and members of the civil society with violence (Masiiwa and Doroh 2011). Three forms of cross-border flows resulted: individuals fleeing political or structural violence and persecution, economic migrants, and visitors/cross-border traders embarking on short trips to buy goods or visit relatives (Kiwanuka and Monson 2009: 27). The emigration trends can be seen in the Table 1 below.

Table 1: Migration trends from 2000 – 2015

Period	Number of Migrants	Percentage (decline or Increase) of Migrants
2015	398, 866.00	0.25%
2010	397, 891.00	1.32%
2005	392, 693.00	4.32%
2000	410, 041.00	4.91%

Source: World Bank (2020)

The decline in the number of emigrants was attributed to the ephemeral economic stability and political tolerance and inclusivity that were ushered in by the inclusive government from 2009 to 2013 (Zimano et al. 2019).

Additionally, the aftermath of the inclusive government gave some sense of stability and people wanted to consolidate the gains of the dollarised economy. The story began changing after 2015, and emigration rose, with the advent of economic under-performance and political persecutions (World Bank 2020).

According to a study conducted by Zanamwe and Devillard (2010), 411,620 emigrants left the country in 2005, mainly to African countries (357,862) and Europe (53,758). The main destination country in Europe was the United Kingdom, whilst in Africa it was Botswana, South Africa and Mozambique in that order. The 2005 outflow was significant in that there was deteriorating food security as a result of the Fast Track Land Reform Programme, Operation Murambatsvina (Restore Order) – which saw many people and informal traders being displaced in the urban areas – and a ZANU-PF landslide election victory in 2005 which quashed people's political hopes (Chilunjika and Uwizeyimana 2015). Zanamwe and Devillard (2010) are of the view that the economic crisis of the 2000s was the main driver of emigration flows. Cross-border migration remains one of the key survival strategies for many households.

Southern Africa has a long history of population movements – mobility has been a central and defining feature of the region's politics, economy and culture. In the past 20 years, an increasing number of people have migrated to escape poverty, seek livelihoods or escape from political upheavals and civil strife, such as the Mozambican and Angolan civil wars – whose effects on regional development continue to be felt to date. The patterns and scale of these population movements are constantly in flux. While we show that issues of immigration control and xenophobic violence are less prominent in popular debates in Botswana, Malawi, Mozambique and Zambia than in South Africa, we note that governments and civil societies in other Southern African countries are not prepared or capacitated to respond to sustained, large-scale flows of migrants such as those originating from Zimbabwe over recent years (Kiwanuka and Monson 2009).

According to Kiwanuku and Monson (ibid.) attitudes to Zimbabwean migrants appear to be more positive in Malawi, Mozambique and Zambia than in Botswana. The authors suggest that the local populations in Malawi, Mozambique and Zambia were perceived by Zimbabweans as more friendly and helpful than those in Botswana, and evidence shows that many communities support Zimbabwean migrants with food, employment and accommodation. This might be as a result of the historical ties that were shared between Zimbabwe, Zambia, Mozambique and South Africa where people would migrate from their respective countries to work in Zimbabwean mines and farms. Apparently, some Zambians, Malawians and Mozambicans are still staying in Zimbabwe and some have dual citizenship and thus belong to either country.2 This might contribute to the warm reception that they render to Zimbabwean migrants. Additionally, most immigrants are migrant workers and are employed either formally or more often informally in their countries of destination. Immigration thus plays a key role in the destination countries' economic development (OECD/ ILO 2018).

Although the literature consistently observes that, second to South Africa, Botswana is the primary destination for Zimbabwean emigrants, the quality of data available in Malawi, Mozambique and Zambia appears too poor to reliably assess the scale of Zimbabwean migration across the four countries (Masiiwa and Doroh 2011).

Botswana appears to issue more work permits to Zimbabweans than any of the other three countries, and a relatively large number of Zimbabweans reportedly work within its government structures (Tevera and Crush 2010). Policy there is silent on the topic of migrant and refugee healthcare, and only nationals receive free anti-retroviral therapy (ART). The official responsible for security and migrants in the Office of the President reported that this was because the state does not yet have adequate resources to provide ART to the full population of citizens living with HIV (ibid.; Kiwanuka and Monson 2009).

Pophiwa (2018) pointed to the impact of the Zimbabwean crisis on neighbouring countries, which tends to emphasise the burden of hosting Zimbabwean 'migrants'. The influx of migrants has exerted untold pressure on the host destinations' resources and amenities, leading to competition for employment opportunities, finance, and educational and health facilities.

In countries with high unemployment, such as Zimbabwe, cross-border trade is often the only income-generating option. Such traders are predominantly unemployed women who regularly visit neighbouring countries to buy merchandise such as clothes and groceries for personal consumption and for resale. Additionally, although Zimbabweans' primary reason for migration was livelihood seeking, access to medical was also a

---

2 'Zimbabwe: Diaspora Remittances Stagnant at USD1.85bln – World Bank', *allAfrica*, 20 December 2018.

consideration (Chroma 2020). Emergency medical services are provided free in some countries for migrants in critical condition and with no means to pay. This has given rise to pregnant women from Zimbabwe seeking childbirth services in Botswana and Mozambique.

Trends and key drivers of migration

In Zimbabwe's high migrant sending areas (including Chiredzi, Chipinge, Gwanda, Bulilima and Plumtree), more than 80% of households have at least one family member who is an irregular migrant (Chitambara 2019; Pophiwa 2018; Chimbodza 2012). Regarding the nature of migrants leaving Zimbabwe during this time, the largest group consists of unskilled workers, who choose nearby destinations such as South Africa. They tend to work for relatively short periods and in menial jobs, for example as farm labourers, domestic works and casual workers.

De Villiers and Weda (2017), describe some of this group as 'survival migrants', fleeing political persecution. More broadly, the profile of migrants from South Africa is mixed, consisting of both those seeking long-term refugee status, and those seeking temporary economic opportunities. Zimbabweans represented 54% of all new asylum seekers in South Africa in 2008 and two-thirds of all new asylum applicants in 2009. More than 50% of the Zimbabwean migrants are seeking economic opportunities (Pophiwa 2018). In the process they then apply for asylum so that they enjoy some degree of protection, immunity and stability whilst they pursue economic prospects and opportunities.

Table 2 shows that the highest proportion of migrants (48.4%) moved alone, followed by those who moved as an entire household (21.6%) and those who moved with parents (11%). With the exception of migrants who moved with those not related to them, all categories were dominated by females.

Zimbabwean trends and key drivers

Although migration in Zimbabwe is strongly associated with poverty (Ranga 2015; Dzingirai et al. 2015), it also includes professionals. 20,000 health care professionals are believed to have left the country since the turn of the millennium, to work in the United Kingdom, New Zealand, Australia and Namibia. The Middle East and Asia are not professionals' preferred destination, except for specific sectors such as engineering, aviation and insurance. Zanamwe and Devillard (2010) and Chikanda and Dodson (2015) provide excellent discussions of this brain drain.

Table 2: Distribution of migrants by company on migration and sex, Zimbabwe 2019 LFCLS (ZimStat 2019)

Company on migration	Number			%			%			Sex (Overall)
	Male	Female	Total	Male	Female	Total	Male	Within Female		Total
Alone	406,764	425,929	832,693	48.8	51.2	100	51.6	45.6		48.4
Entire household	180,275	190,814	371,089	48.6	51.4	100	22.9	20.5		21.6
Spouse	20,478	28,285	48,763	42	58	100	2.6	3		2.8
Son/daughter	2,378	65,186	67,564	3.5	96.5	100	0.3	7		3.9
Parent(s)	85,479	106,531	192,009	44.5	55.5	100	10.8	11.4		11.2
Brother/sister	42,709	47,105	89,814	47.6	52.4	100	5.4	5		5.2
Other relative	21,140	23,076	44,216	47.8	52.2	100	2.7	2.5		2.6
Not related	1,362	54	1,416	96.2	3.8	100	0.2	0		0.1
Part of household	28,189	46,052	74,242	38	62	100	3.6	4.9		4.3
Total	788,774	933,032	1,721,806	45.8	54.2	100	100	100		100

Health professionals

Zimbabwe has been negatively affected by the emigration of a large number of its medical doctors. Chikanda and Dodson (ibid.) note that the number who have left the country is difficult to estimate since the country does not keep such records. Most of those who initially migrated were more experienced nurses with skills that were marketable abroad, leaving behind junior and less experienced staff (Chikanda, 2010).

Western countries have sought to solve their nursing shortages by aggressively recruiting professionals from developing countries such as Zimbabwe. According to Chikanda and Dodson (2015) Zimbabwe has lost a substantial number of its medical personnel to countries such as the UK, United States, Canada and South Africa. Zimbabwean migrants now view these countries not as places of temporary economic opportunity but rather as places to stay and build a future for themselves and their families. These losses have brought remittances, return migration and other diaspora engagement initiatives. The better remunerations that migrants earn are the basis for remittances that are sent home to support families and communities (Chikanda 2010). Remittance flows benefit both the migrants' households and the non-recipient ones through the multiplier effects of spending.

Teachers

Zimbabweans constitute the largest group of migrant teachers in South Africa (DHET 2013). According to de Villiers and Weda (2017) South Africa was already home to 10,000 Zimbabwean teachers by 2004, of whom 4,000 were qualified science and mathematics teachers. An estimated 47% of the Zimbabwean teachers in South Africa end up working in other sectors (ibid.).

Current remittances flows in Africa

Remittance flows Sub-Saharan African countries are expected drop by 23.1% to US$37 billion in 2020 in the wake of the COVID-19 economic crisis.[3] In 2019, flows dipped by 0.5% to $48 billion. Nigeria, which has a sizeable diaspora across the world, is by far the largest recipient of remittance flows (US$23.8 billion in 2019) followed by Ghana ($3.5 billion) and Kenya ($2.8 billion). In South Sudan, remittances of $1.3 billion accounted for 34% of its GDP, the highest in the region (ibid.).

---

3 'Remittances from migrants to African countries will plunge by nearly a quarter this year', *Quartz Africa*, 24 April 2020.

Top 10 highest remittance receiving countries in Africa (US$ billion), 2019

1	Nigeria	$23,8
2	Ghana	$3,5
3	Kenya	$2,8
4	Senegal	$2,5
5	DRC	$1,8
6	Zimbabwe	$1,7
7	Uganda	$1,3
8	South Sudan	$1,3
9	Mali	$1,0
10	South Africa	$0.9

Source: World Bank (2019)

While some of migrant income is remitted formally, through for example transfer agencies and, more recently, mobile banking, much of it is through informal networks based on trust (Bracking and Sachikonye 2010). The use of 'malaitshas', personal couriers, relatives and religious networks are noteworthy forms of remitting income and goods. Because they are based on trust, these forms have their own risks, but they remain attractive to the poor migrants who often cannot afford to use formal channels (Dzingirai et al. 2014).

While it is true that much remitted income is invested in non-productive areas such as funerals, weddings, and of course food (Dzingirai et al. 2014), some is directed towards economic production, including purchasing of livestock, land and small businesses (Bracking and Sachikonye, 2006; Zanamwe and Devillard, 2010).

Remittances and the Zimbabwean case

World Bank estimates that migrant remittances through official channels amounted to US$17 million in 1980, increasing to US$33 million in 1982, and US$44 million in 1994. "Zimbabwe received more than US$505 million in international remittances from January to June 2019 and indications are that the annual figure will fall slightly short of the US$1,1 billion received in 2018. Of the 2018 figure, US$620 million was the share for diaspora remittances. In 2017, international remittances were US$1,4 billion while diaspora remittances were US$699 million (Diaspora remittances share was down from US$779 million recorded in 2016)".[4]

According to Dzingirai et al. (2015) remittance behaviour varies between male and female migrants, with men tending to remit more than women. This may reflect different work opportunities and pay structures: the most common occupation for migrant men is skilled construction, whereas for women it is domestic service (ibid.).

Zanamwe and Devillard (2010) suggest that remittances bring positive benefits to the country if they are transferred through formal channels and are invested in productive economic activities. They further argue that remittance transfers through informal channels such as *malaitshas,* which are used for consumption, bring limited economic benefit to the country. Masiiwa and Doroh (2011) stated that about 72% of Zimbabweans in the diaspora send remittances to relatives and friends back home and this is mostly done through informal channels. The recipients of the remittances use the money for food (41%), education (12%), rentals (10%), health (7%), and clothing (7%).

According to the IOM (2010) many Zimbabweans who migrated for economic reasons continued to support their family members through financial and in-kind transfers during the economic decline of the past decade. The preferred investment areas are immovable property, motor and transport, agriculture and mining. Those in the unskilled and illegal categories tend to rely on the informal channels to remit consumption goods such as groceries, foodstuffs and clothing.

The COVID-19 pandemic has crippled the economies of rich and poor countries alike. For many low-income and fragile states, the economic shock was, and is still, magnified by the loss of remittances. Zimbabwean migrants stimulate economic growth and development in areas of destination, transit and origin through their labour, skills transfer, consumption and investments. Their remittances, as argued by FAO (2020), also make significant contributions to food security, human capital, rural development and overall GDP in the sending countries. According to FAO there was a 23% decline in remittances flows into the Sub-Saharan Africa as a result of economic downturns, restrictions in movement and challenges in sending transfers.

The COVID-19 pandemic saw Zimbabwean migrant workers being more exposed to vulnerable situations and the loss of employment. A

---

4 'Diaspora remittances can boost Zim economy', *Zimbabwe Independent*, 7 February 2020.

considerable number of those employed in low skilled professions with a high level of informality were the hard hit owing to limited savings and lack of access to social security. Strict lockdown measures imposed by the governments across the globe, implied immediate job losses and restricted capacity for migrant workers to engage in economic activities. The pandemic saw borders being closed from March 2020, making it difficult and expensive for migrants to remit money and goods.

Despite the fact that consumables were hard to send across the borders, monetary remittances became a commonly used avenue; with relaxation of the lockdown restrictions in September and October 2020, people could now easily access hard currency sent by their migrant relatives beyond the borders.

Export of goods and services

According to Meagher (2003) the strangulation of popular livelihoods in the context of rising unemployment and nose-diving real incomes in developing countries has encouraged increased participation in transborder activities as a means of income generation. Many of the African continent's official borders and unofficial crossing points are hives of activity as commodities flow in several directions to ensure the survival of communities that live across them (Pophiwa 2018). The Common Market for Eastern and Southern Africa (COMESA) and the Southern Africa Development Community (SADC), by enabling income generation, help preserve lives and sustain families in Zimbabwe in the face of its current challenges (Kiwanuka and Monson 2009). The COMESA Treaty guarantees free movement of goods and services wholly produced within member states. It allows free entry by traders from member states, and waives custom duties on products produced in member countries.

Under the Treaty, Zimbabweans may enter Malawi or Zambia and engage in cross-border trade without the burden of taxes (ibid.). Because all four countries (South Africa included) have ratified the SADC Protocol on Free Trade, which offers similar advantages to those of the COMESA Treaty, few tariffs and non-tariff barriers apply to Zimbabwean traders in Botswana or Mozambique either. This has encouraged circular migration, i.e. the movement of people across the border of a neighbouring country for a period of less than one day.

As the economy declined and basic goods became scarce, Zimbabwe witnessed a growth in the number of day-trippers to neighbouring countries. Beitbridge experiences the highest volume, into neighbouring South Africa, followed by the Plumtree border into Botswana and the Nyamapanda border into Mozambique (Zanamwe and Devillard 2010). These arrangements promote and improve business opportunities and profits in the countries concerned, and by facilitating income generation also help preserve lives and sustain families in Zimbabwe. Most people are not required to have official travel documents, as they are given gate passes which are stamped at the border (Masiiwa and Doroh 2010; Zanamwe and Devillard, 2010).

Foreign direct investment, corporate governance

Whilst the diaspora makes a substantial contribution to remittances, it is not clear whether enough is invested in the home country to stimulate economic growth and create employment (Masiiwa and Doroh 2011). Besides, the Zimbabwean diaspora is not involved in any systematic or important trade, mainly because of a lack of awareness of the market situation at home. In April 2008 the government established the Migration and Development Unit (MDU) in the Ministry of Economic Planning and Investment Promotion in order to improve the coordination of migration and diaspora activities.

The Unit works closely with the International Organization for Migration (IOM) which has also provided the office, equipment, stationery and a vehicle as part of its capacity building (Masiiwa and Doroh 2011). It spearheads the national migration and development agenda on a daily basis. The ministry responsible has also formulated a Migration Management and Diaspora Policy, with technical assistance from IOM. The volatile economic situation in Zimbabwe appeared to discourage the diaspora from extensive trade activities. Further impediments to trade were given as the lack of adequate capital to procure high volumes of tradable goods that can be sold at a profit, political uncertainty, exclusion from the socio-political processes, limited channels of investment and trade, inadequate market related information and limited institutions dealing with diaspora issues.

Investment, trade policy and tax policy

Throughout the world, the diaspora plays an important role in the development of home countries' economies through remittances, skills and technology transfers, investments, trade, and the creation of social and professional networks that advance the countries' development. Most Zimbabweans in the diaspora are investing and trading in their home country. For example, many in China, the UK and South Africa have opened grocery shops, boutiques, and hardware shops, where they employ either their relatives or reliable employees to run the businesses on their behalf.

However, Zimbabwe lacks institutions specifically dedicated to facilitating diaspora investment and trade, and to ensuring that people do not fall prey to fraudulent activities, and the diaspora is concerned about the poor access to investment and trade related information (Masiiwa and Doroh 2011); the Zimbabwe Investment Authority (ZIA), Zimbabwe National Chamber of Commerce (ZNCC) and Confederation of Zimbabwe Industries (CZI) are supposed to provide such information (ibid.).

A stable economic situation is a prerequisite for investment. The macroeconomic environment needs to improve first before people in the diaspora can feel confident to invest in Zimbabwe. Remittances for 2020 are estimated be well under US$1.9 billion, the same as in 2017 and 2016.[5] This is down from a peak of US$2 billion in 2015.

Policy Framework

There are a number of government ministries dealing with migration and diaspora issues, including the Ministry of Labour and Social Services, Ministry of Foreign Affairs, Ministry of Education, Sport, Arts and Culture, Ministry of Regional Integration and International Cooperation, Ministry of Higher and Tertiary Education and the Ministry of Youth Development, Indigenisation and Empowerment. These have played a crucial role in enacting the following migration and diaspora related policies.

National Diaspora Policy

Zimbabwe developed the National Diaspora Policy with the United Nation Migration Agency Support. The main themes of the policy are capacity building, migration and development. Zimbabwe convened a high level discussion to develop the country's 2017-2022 National Diaspora Policy Implementation Action Plan with support from the International Organization for Migration and the European Union. The Plan serves as a framework for engaging with the Zimbabwean diaspora worldwide. Eighty participants took part from government ministries, the UN and the private sector, as well as diaspora representatives and other non-state actors. Policy

---

5 'Zimbabwe: Diaspora Remittances Stagnant at USD1.85bln – World Bank', *allAfrica*, 20 December 2018.

interventions can help improve the investment and trade in the country by the diaspora (Masiiwa and Doroh 2011).

The operationalisation of the 2016 National Diaspora Policy comes against a background of increasing government acknowledgement of the potential of the diaspora in contributing towards national development. The action plan comprises eight priority areas that relate to policies and legislation, the intra-governmental-diaspora relationship, institutional engagement, diaspora relationship, institutional engagement, diaspora investment, remittances, national socio-economic development, and diaspora rights. The adoption of the Policy and the subsequent establishment of the Diaspora Directorate are testimony to the government's commitment to promote diaspora engagement.

National Labour Migration Policy

The National Labour Migration Policy was formulated to make it easier for lower skilled people to seek work abroad and offer them social protection, while at the same time strengthening mechanisms for harnessing remittances for economic development. In addition to establishing sustainable and inclusive labour migration management systems that promote good governance, the policy also seeks to protect the welfare of thousands of Zimbabweans living abroad and implement strategies to deal with the challenges posed by migration of all forms.

Through this policy, the government seeks to maximise the benefits of inward and outward labour migration for national development, including through remittances and investment promotion and functional labour market information systems. It is difficult to gauge the effectiveness of this policy as most labour migrants are working illegally.

Regional and International Policy Frameworks

Migration management policies operate at two levels: international and national. At the international level, a further distinction can be made between universal instruments protecting migrants' rights, regional instruments and mechanisms organising a cooperation framework between African and, more specifically, Southern African countries, and bilateral agreements concluded by Zimbabwe for the regulation of migration flows (Zanamwe and Devillard 2009). The international framework protecting migrants is found in two places, namely international human rights law and specific instruments such as the ILO Conventions Nos. 97 and 143, and the International Convention on the Rights of All Migrant Workers and Members of Their Families. Therefore, migrants, as non-nationals, are generally entitled to the same human rights as citizens.

The availability of permits allowing legal entry eases pressure on the migration system. These permits include: 90-day visitors' permits for SADC citizens in Malawi, Mozambique, Zambia and Botswana; one-day, 50km border passes in Mozambique, Zambia and Botswana; COMESA permits in Malawi, Mozambique and Zambia (Kiwanuka and Monson, 2009). Similarly, Zanamwe and Devillard (2010) are of the view that the capacity of the government to minimise the negative consequences of migration while maximising its positive effects is constrained by the lack of a comprehensive and coherent legal, institutional and policy framework for implementing migration processes in an integrated manner. They further state that the limitations are exacerbated by the lack of adequate data and analysis of the factors driving migration.

Political participation

Every investor in the world considers the political situation in a country before investing and Zimbabweans in the diaspora are no exception. The diaspora should not only be expected to invest in Zimbabwe but should also be allowed to freely participate in the political processes in the country. Granting them dual citizenship and voters' rights would help address some of their major concerns. Experiences in other countries (Brazil, the Philippines, Mexico, Peru, Jamaica, Egypt, Nigeria, Ghana, Burundi, India and Senegal) have shown that allowing dual citizenship improves the level of participation of the diaspora in investment. Opinions from the diaspora should always be sought whenever issues of importance are debated in Parliament (Masiiwa and Doroh 2011). To enable the full and free participation of the diaspora in domestic politics, the necessary infrastructure should be put in place. This includes developing an interactive parliamentary website where the diaspora can freely express its views, and enabling Zimbabwean embassies to handle the diaspora votes. The encouragement of people to freely participate in the political processes at home would stimulate investment.

Bilateral agreements

Bilateral labour agreements (BLAs) are arrangements between states, regions and public institutions that provide for the recruitment and employment of short-term or long-term foreign labour (Zimano et al. 2019). BLAs are usually concluded for three reasons: economic reasons, in order to organise a match between supply and demand for labour; political reasons, in order to promote friendly relations between states by encouraging the orderly movement of labour; and development reasons, in order to counter the 'brain drain'.

Zimbabwe has concluded very few BLAs. In the 2000s, the country had an agreement with Cuba for the recruitment of Cuban health professionals in order to limit the negative consequence of the emigration of national health professionals; the agreement is apparently yet to be implemented. At present, the only applicable BLA appears to be the recent one concluded with South Africa for the facilitation of recruitment of labour for commercial farms in Limpopo Province in South Africa.

Concluding remarks

Migration has long been used as a way for households to seek work, improve their livelihoods and raise their incomes, as well as to escape more extreme situations of persecution, conflict and hunger (Dzingirai et al. 2015). Pophiwa (2018) argued that the poor Zimbabwean migrants in cities such as Johannesburg are living in squalid spaces to eke out a living. For the purpose of facilitating humanitarian intervention for Zimbabwean migrants and better managing the impacts on their own citizens, governments in the region should acknowledge the humanitarian nature of migration from Zimbabwe, and encourage services targeted at undocumented Zimbabweans as a humanitarian response to forced migration rather than discouraging them.

- Economic growth is affected both negatively and positively by different forms of migration. It is imperative that policies be crafted to help in harnessing the favourable benefits of migration whilst minimising the adverse effects.

- Policies on migration should help engender confidence among the people who have crossed the borders to contribute towards economic development back home. In light of this, there is need for the formalisation of the remittances so that the gains are directly received by migrants' relatives, with the state benefiting through taxes. The COVID-19 pandemic has exposed the need for the digitisation of service provision, so that remittances are not hindered by lockdown restrictions.

- People in the diaspora should be allowed to vote, as this engenders a sense of inclusivity and belonging; they should not be alienated from the local and national developmental processes.
- All governments should mainstream migration issues in their social development policies, specifically in terms of health, welfare, housing and education, in order to incorporate migrant issues in the planning processes (Kiwanuka and Monson, 2009). Given the diverse nature of Zimbabwean migration flows, and the lack of active local partners capable of assisting Zimbabwean communities, it will be difficult to coordinate a regional humanitarian intervention that will adequately address the needs of Zimbabwean migrants.

References

Bracking, S. and L. Sachikonye (2010) 'Migrant Remittances and Household Wellbeing in Urban Zimbabwe', *International Migration*, 48(5), pp. 203-227.

Chikanda, A. (2010) 'Nursing the Health System: The Migration of Health Professionals from Zimbabwe', in J. Crush and D. Tevera (eds) *Zimbabwe's Exodus: Crisis, Migration, Survival.* Cape Town: Southern Africa Migration Programme; Ottawa: International Development Research Centre.

——— and B. Dodson (2015) 'Medical Migration from Zimbabwe: Towards New Solutions?', in N.I. Luginaah and R. Bezner-Kerr (eds) *Geographies of Health and Development.* Farnham: Ashgate.

Chilunjika, A. and D.E. Uwizeyimana (2015) 'Shifts in the Land Reform Discourse from 1980 to present', *Journal of Public* Affairs, 8(3), pp. 130-144.

Chimbodza, A. (2012) 'From Brain Drain to Brain Gain: Addressing Human Capital Needs for Post Crisis Zimbabwe's Capacity Building'. MPhil thesis, University of Pennsylvania.

Chitambara, P. (2019) 'Remittances, Institutions and Growth in Africa', *International Migration*, 57(5), pp. 56-70.

Crush, J., A. Chikanda and G. Tawodzera (2012) 'The Third Wave: Mixed Migration from Zimbabwe to South Africa'. Southern African Migration Programme, Cape Town.

Dagdemir, Ö., Z. Kartal, R. Tinas and H. Gürbüz (2018) 'The Impact of

Migration on Poverty and Income Distribution in a Rural Region in Turkey', *Remittances Review*, 3(2), pp. 151-176.

Damelang, A. and A. Haas (2012) 'The Benefits of Migration', *European Societies*, 14(3), pp. 362-392.

de Villiers, R. and Z. Weda (2017) 'Zimbabwean teachers in South Africa: A transient greener pasture', *Southern African Journal of Education*, 37(3) pp. 1-9.

Department of Higher Education & Training (DHET) (2013) 'Evaluation of Qualification Sets Submitted by Migrant Teachers in 2010'. Pretoria: DHET.

Dzingirai, V., P. Mutopo and L. Landau (2014) 'Confirmations, Coffins and Corn: Kinship, Social Networks and Remittances from South Africa to Zimbabwe'. 'Migrating out of Poverty' Research Programme, University of Sussex.

Dzingirai, V., E-M. Egger, L. Landau, J. Litchfield, P. Mutopo and K. Nyikahadzoi, (2015) 'Migrating out of Poverty in Zimbabwe'. Working Paper 29. 'Migrating out of Poverty' Research Programme, University of Sussex.

FAO (2020) 'Migrant Workers and the COVID-19 Pandemic'. Rome: FAO.

Griswold, D. (2018) 'The Benefits of Immigration: Addressing Key Myths'. Policy Brief, George Mason University.

IOM (2010) 'Migration in Zimbabwe: A Country Profile 2009'. Geneva: IOM.

Kiwanuka, M. and T. Monson (2009) 'Zimbabwean Migration into Southern Africa: New Trends and Responses'. Forced Migration Studies Programme, University of the Witwatersrand.

Macrotrends (2020) *Zimbabwe Immigration Statistics 1960-2020*. https://www.macrotrends.net/countries/ZWE/zimbabwe/immigration-statistics

Masiiwa, M. and B. Doroh (2011) *Harnessing the Diaspora Potential for Socio-Economic Development in Zimbabwe: Investment, Trade and Participation in Political Processes*. Harare: Institute of Development Studies, University of Zimbabwe,.

Mawowa, S. and A. Matongo (2010) 'Inside Zimbabwe's Roadside Currency Trade: The "World Bank" of Bulawayo', *Journal of Southern*

African Studies, 36(2), pp. 319-337.

Meagher, K. (2003) 'A Back Door to Globalisation? Structural Adjustment, Globalisation & Transborder Trade in West Africa', *Review of African Political Economy*, 30(95), pp. 57-75.

OECD/ILO (2018) *How Immigrants Contribute to Developing to Developing Countries' Economies*. Paris: OECD Publishing.

Pophiwa, N. (2018) 'Cross-border shopping by Zimbabweans in Musina: Meanings, modalities and encounters (c. 2000-2016)'. PhD thesis, University of KwaZulu-Natal.

Progressive Teachers Union of Zimbabwe (PTUZ) (2008) 'PTUZ highlights critical issues plaguing education system to Ministry'. Harare: Kubatana.net.

Ranga, B. (2015) 'The role of politics in the migration of Zimbabwean teachers to South Africa', *Development Southern Africa*, 32(2), pp. 258-273.

Tevera, D. and J. Crush (2010) 'The New Brain Drain from Zimbabwe'. Migration Policy Series No. 29. Cape Town, Southern African Migration Project.

World Bank (2003) *Global Development Finance 2003*. Washington, DC: World Bank.

⸻ (2016) *Migration and Remittances Factbook 2016*. Washington, DC: World Bank.

⸻ (2020) *WB Predicts Sharpest Decline of Remittances in Recent History*. Washington, DC: World Bank.

Zanamwe, L. and A. Devillard (2010) *Migration in Zimbabwe: A country profile 2009,* Harare: ZimStat, IOM.

Zimano, F.R., D. Chimanikire and A. Chilunjika (2019) 'Border Management Systems' intelligence and annotations on existing transit challenges in Zimbabwe', in S. Muqayi and C. Manyeruke, *Dynamics of Contemporary Border Management in Zimbabwe: Challenges, Benefits and Prospects*. London: Adonis and Abbey Publishers.

Zimbabwe National Statistics Agency (ZimStat) (2019) *2019 Labour Force and Child Labour Survey*. Harare: ZimStat.

7

Social Exclusion of Women and Youth and Development since Independence

Rekopantswe Mate

Introduction: why social exclusion matters

Social exclusion is taken here to refer to experiences of the marginalised, those left of out of socio-economic and political processes and institutions through unemployment, underemployment and poverty (Leysens 2006). It includes not being able to earn an income or earning erratically, lacking education and skills, being self-employed, and doing informal sector work. Social exclusion is therefore about disenfranchisement. It points to isolation, and the inability to participate in socio-cultural, economic and political activities. It is about unfulfilled citizenship rights, as excluded people cannot exercise choices as citizens or consumers.

Social exclusion is multidimensional, relational, and is linked to poverty and therefore to social policy (Boon and Farnsworth 2011). Although political scientists fear that generalised social exclusion can lead to unrest and revolts, Leysens (2006) argues that in fact the majority of socially excluded persons in Southern Africa are engrossed in survival and adaptation to unfolding challenges of their circumstances. They are least likely to engage in revolt. Our concern therefore has to be with social exclusion as denial of citizenship rights, as life lived without dignity.

Demographically, women constitute 52% of the population and youth around 40-44%. However, either as separate groups, or together, they lack the political, economic and cultural clout to influence decision-making because of socio-cultural factors of gerontocracy (age domination) and patriarchy (male domination). These two structures of inequality work together and predate independence. They pervade all sectors and justify the exclusion and subordination of women and young people. Marginalisation based on gerontocracy and patriarchy are taken for granted by ordinary citizens and defended as 'our culture'. Thus to meaningfully undo the social exclusion of young people and women we need a thoroughgoing critique of 'our culture' and the accepted way of life that allots roles by gender and age, in addition to legislative and policy reforms.

This chapter discusses the social exclusion of women and youth in four areas: work and employment, access to resources, political participation and decision-making, and education. All four areas are included in the Sustainable Development Goals (SDGs) and mentioned in several 1990s UN conferences that spawned the them. Each sector is discussed separately, including explanations of its significance and a discussion of why the social exclusion persists.

Access to schooling and education achievements

Education's role in development cannot be underestimated. It is defined as a right by the Ministry of Primary and Secondary Education, as well as by the SDGs. It is about transforming the individual and society as a whole. It is part of development as well as a means to development by capacitating citizens to participate in development as workers, consumers and activists in civil society. At independence, it was seen as crucial for creating an equitable and changed Zimbabwe (Zvobgo 1987). However, the post-independence quantitative bias in education achievements such as the speedy establishment of new schools and the expansion of enrolments and teacher training are at the core of the marginalisation of young people (MacKenzie 1988; Johnson 1990; Pape 1998). Despite high literacy rates, the declining quality of education since 1980 – seen in low pass rates at O Level (Abraham 2003; CSO 2001) and a focus on reading competences instead of critical thinking (Johnson 1990) – have remained a challenge. The O Level pass rate plunged below 20% in 1985, 1986 and 1999 (CSO 2001: 42). Official statistics up to 2017 show that the O Level pass rate has consistently remained around 20%, although it goes up slightly in some years (ZimStat 2018: 31). Furthermore, the premium placed on academic subjects at the expense of practical subjects (Pape 1998) limits alternatives for less academically gifted students. Gender disaggregated information on O level pass rates is not available. There are no comprehensive tracer studies that document what happens to young people who fail O Level exams (Grant 2003).

Other dynamics that fuel marginalisation include gender issues, the rural-urban divide, the impact of HIV and AIDS, and now COVID-19 restrictions. Gender parity in primary school enrolments and completion rates has not been sustained in secondary and tertiary education. From 1991-2000, female students constituted 40-45% of total enrolment in Form 4 (CSO 2001: 34). In the same period,, female enrolment was 35% at the University of Zimbabwe, 19% at the National University of Science and Technology, 46% at Africa University and close to 50% at Solusi University (ibid.: 44).

Table 1: Female and male enrolments in teacher training colleges

Gender	1994	1999	2004	2009	2014	2017
Male	8 375	9 280	8 483	3 193	6 087	9 088
Female	8 043	9 733	10 502	7 624	12 705	19 522
Total	16 418	19 013	18 985	10 817	18 792	28 610

Source: Adapted from ZimStat (2018: 33-34).

It is important to note that during since the late 1990s, morale in teaching declined to unprecedented levels because of economic and political crises. Consequently, women dominate training in a profession that is in decline, thus channelling them to disempowerment. Teachers have been engaged in protracted industrial action, calling for higher wages.

Female enrolment in technical colleges is 30%, in vocational colleges 21%, and in agricultural colleges 35%. Throughout the 2000s, male biases in technical and vocational training colleges have remained (ZimStat 2018: 49-61). To the extent that education is concerned with the development of human resources, it has benefited men more than women.

In the predominantly rural provinces of Mashonaland Central, Mashonaland West, and Matabeleland South and North there were comparatively few students enrolled in secondary school between 1990 and 2000 (CSO 2001). Between 2006 and 2017, this trend was largely still in evidence (ZimStat 2018: 24). Widely acknowledged rural-urban differences in access to school show that differences in availability, quality of facilities and trained teachers impinges on education outcomes. Rural district council and community schools, the majority of which are in rural areas, perform poorly in O Level exams compared to government, mission, trust and urban council schools, because of the latter's superior facilities, and ability to attract and retain qualified teachers (Bennell and Ncube 1994).

These differences have implications for who have access to university education. Using fathers' employment as a proxy for background, a study done by Bennell and Ncube (ibid.) shows that most students' fathers were employed in the public sector; the students had attended the better and relatively more expensive government and mission schools. Children of peasants who went to rural district council and community schools were few. Bennell and Ncube concluded that university education served to consolidate class differences. Perhaps the situation changed after 1990 when more universities were established. There are no known analyses of enrolments by rural or urban origins and socio-economic backgrounds since the mid-1990s.

The increase in the number of orphaned and vulnerable children (OVCs) during the 1990s and 2000s saw the government introduce the Basic Education Assistance Module (BEAM) to pay fees for children from poor backgrounds. Tuition did not extend to universities though. BEAM was funded partly from the AIDS levy. Later, donors that fund children's issues also contributed to the fund. However, mismanagement, poor community participation and targeting, delayed disbursements of funds and eventual donor withdrawal has undermined the sustainability of BEAM since about 2010 (TARSC 2012). Table 2 shows the number of OVCs and beneficiaries from BEAM between 2014 and 2018 (GoZ 2019). It is not clear if the benefits were continuous or one-off.

The table 2 shows that the coverage of BEAM has not been comprehensive. Given the fact that students drop out of school because of financial constraints, pregnancy and early marriage, the limited coverage of BEAM is a cause for concern. Furthermore, more males benefit from BEAM than females (ibid.). The reasons are likely to do with household level decision-making. This indicates that female OVC are at higher risk of exclusion from education assistance.

Table 2: Number of OVCs benefiting from BEAM

	ECD	Primary school	Secondary school
Number of OVCs	107,134	584,114	318,695
Number benefiting from BEAM	-	384,057	170,636
Difference (not benefiting)	107,134	200,057	148,059

Source: Adapted from GoZ (2019: xi-xiii)

Since the 1990s the number of universities increased, as did graduate unemployment as more students graduate. There were 17 state and private universities in 2020. They produce an estimated 30,000 degree holders per year. However, many graduate to chronic unemployment (Gukurume 2017) leading to cynicism about the utility of degrees vis-à-vis employability.

Contrary to expectations at independence such as expressed by Zvobgo (1987), endemic unemployment has stalled aspirations for upward social mobility through wage work as well as change from peasant livelihoods to skilled and professional work. ZimStat (2020: 36) says that 16% (566,449) of the potential labour is currently unemployed. Furthermore, slightly over a million individuals are counted as 'discouraged job seekers' who have failed to find work for a long period of time. The search for solutions is on-going but is mostly debated with few practical solutions. Still, the education system is blamed for using an inappropriate, out-dated, irrelevant or Eurocentric curriculum (Grant 2003).

The idea that there is need to adapt the school and university curricula to meet changing labour market demands dates back to the Nziramasanga Commission of 1999. It assumes that education is an independent variable in national development. The skills it spawns are used by different sectors of the economy, thereby driving development. The reality is more complex, and the curriculum could well be a dependent variable. Examples from other countries show that industry can also influence curricular changes by either identifying training needs or training school leavers through apprenticeships. Policies on the latter became confused in the late 1980s as the government tried to gain control of manpower development by sometimes barring sectors from certifying skills, or by interfering in training programmes (Dansereau 2000: 230-34). The challenges and arguments over education and skills training remained largely unresolved, for several reasons.

Firstly, Zimbabweans have a negative attitude towards a two-track secondary education (one for academics and another for practical subjects for less academically gifted). The negative attitude originates in the colonial era when non-academic subjects were offered to Africans. Thus, people perceived practical subjects as channelling young people to inferior, manual work that was also comparatively lowly paid (Pape 1998). Although after independence there were efforts to introduce 'education with production', these were unsuccessful, probably because of the weight of negativity (Pape 1998).

Secondly, with pass rates hovering around 20% since independence (CSO 2001), there is little policy attention paid and resources dedicated to the vast majority who fail O Level exams. In a study of Bulawayo, Grant (2003) noted that young people who failed their O Levels found themselves stuck at home unable to get work, or to access guidance about finding work or training. Parents too were frustrated; they were unable to find tuition for children to repeat secondary education in order to get into vocational or technical colleges, and they lacked advice about how to help their children. The Bulawayo Municipality's youth centres ran training programmes but had a long waiting list, could not expand their enrolments nor courses, and were generally underfunded. This indicates that the 80% without O Levels are not catered for. There are no institutions within the ministries of education or outside that cater for training or education needs of youths who are less academically inclined.

Thirdly, in the 1990s, Zimbabwe experimented with apprenticeship programmes modelled on those in the UK. However, they did not succeed because of mutual distrust between the government and employers. The apprenticeships were funded through the Zimbabwe Manpower Development Fund (ZIMDEF), financed from a surcharge on the wage bill in the private sector. Employers in selected sectors could get a subsidy if they employed and trained school leavers over a three-year period (Nyazema 2010). The government shared the cost with employers at 3:1, 1:1 and 1:3 from the first year to the third year respectively. However, the fund was beset with a lack of transparency and mutual distrust between employers and the government. As noted above, the government was locked in arguments over skills and certification (Dansereau 2000). Eventually, the ministry of higher education was tasked with skills development. It has been preoccupied with less than 20% of young people who proceed to higher education after O Level.

Fourthly, in response to political and economic crises of the 1990s (including factors that led to fast track land reform and after losing the vote in the constitutional reform process in 2000), the government unilaterally and hastily implemented a curriculum review called National and Strategic Studies (NASS). It was intended to be an antidote against supporting the opposition, and a fear that young people who were then called 'born-frees' did not fully appreciate the cost and meaning of the liberation struggle. Among other things, NASS saw the introduction of National Youth Service (NYS) whose successful trainees were promised preferential access in vocational and technical colleges as well as entry-level employment in the civil service.

This did not entail thoroughgoing changes to the economy to expand employment opportunities for all young people, especially those who did not or could not attend the NYS. It was more about rewarding obedience to political elites/elders and silencing critique. It also led to hastily put together reforms in the secondary school history curriculum. Barnes (2007) argues that the 2000 reforms led to a simplification of the history of the liberation struggle and the roles of its heroes and heroines. In addition, assessments were done by answers to short questions, whereas hitherto essay type exams were preferred. The impact of these changes was a reduction in critical analyses, originality in composing arguments and debates among learners (Matereke 2012). The extent to which this creates competences usable in the labour market is open to speculation. To the extent that critical thinking is a core requirement in improving the quality of education, this simplification seems to undermine it.

Furthermore, Matereke (2012:93) argues that the 2000 emergence of what Terence Ranger describes as 'patriotic history' referring to a narrow and simplistic version of the liberation struggle that focused attention on ZANU-PF and Robert Mugabe's exploits and sacrifices at the instigation of pro-ruling party historians, produced a divisive, simplistic and intolerant form of citizenship education. This version of history assumes that 'patriots' uncritically follow ruling party instructions and sentiments, and are pitted against 'traitors'/sell-outs who question ruling party policies through debate and activism. The latter are dismissed, ridiculed, subjected to physical abuse and vitriol as well as violation of their human rights at the hands of patriots often incited by ruling party elites. This has perpetuated violence against dissenters. Youth militias comprised of NYS trainees have been used as instruments of violence aimed at dissenters.

The exploits of youth militias are denied, as they do not belong to any formal organisation, structure of government or the ruling party (McGregor 2013). Thus, rather than citizenship education underwritten by patriotic history ending violence, moral decadence, division and indiscipline it seems to have worsened them by misleading young people into intolerance and rewarding them for it. Patriotic history and its curricular reforms have weakened academic critique and in turn academic quality. Schools now have 'national pledge' recitals performed at the flagpole and to honour the sacrifice of heroes. Meanwhile, the low quality of education in the majority of rural schools festers. The long-term implications of this indoctrination for manpower development and citizenship rights are yet to be assessed.

Fifthly, if the problem is a Eurocentric curriculum, elite flight to trust schools whose exams are still moderated abroad points to a desire for genuinely global and transferable achievements. This perhaps points the spotlight on local incapacitation rather than to an outdated and Eurocentric curriculum. Technical challenges and scandals such as leaked exam papers continue to dog the local school examinations agency (Abraham 2003, and several media sources). The number of unemployed young people from trust schools is not known. This would prove whether or not Eurocentrism is the problem.

Finally, as if the above is not enough, another review of primary and secondary school curriculum was implemented in 2016. It seems to be based more on the patriotic history element than the need to resolve unemployment. It is based on 'the spirit of *unhu/ubuntu/vumunhu*'. Notwithstanding the controversy of its launch, without adequate training for teachers, textbooks and teaching aids, its impact on employability is yet to be seen.

There is another myth that internships and attachments expose students to the world of work thus making them employable. This begs the question of available vacancies in the face of deindustrialisation. To the extent that attachments and internships become institutionalised, they are a form of volunteerism, which is increasingly seen as signalling commitment to work. Employers like internees who are a source of free labour while some university students believe that they allow them to establish networks with employers. The programmes are yet to be evaluated for effectiveness.

With the education sector privileging academic subjects at the expense of non-academic disciplines in sports and trades, and given the low pass rates in academic subjects, a lot of young people are marginalised. When unemployed, such young people are treated with suspicion. Many resort to do-it yourself (DIY) survival strategies such as hustling (Jones 2010; Kamete 2008) or the performing arts, again without training or support. While trying to eke out a living from the latter, acceptance by the mainstream is challenging for the vast majority of young people who follow the DIY approach. They run the risk of being seen as subversive, work averse and lazy. The creative arts are seen as inferior, as careers of the last resort.

Forty years into independence there are no schools that train young people in acting, script writing, dancing, composing music and playing music instruments. Nollywood, the expansive Nigerian film and entertainment industry that had its origins among unemployed youth, without government or donor aid during the depth of economic crisis in the 1980s, should be an inspiration (Ezeonu 2013). Young Nigerians used simple hand-held camcorders, improvised sets, wardrobe, script writing, editing and distributing but created a multimillion-dollar cultural industry in the process. Nollywood has created millions of jobs in studios and for local entrepreneurs. Furthermore, universities are capitalising on Nollywood's growth by offering training in related disciplines. This shows that there is scope for the DIY approach to offer a solution where decision-makers are open to persuasion and do not assume that youth are ignorant or that the education sector drives economic development. In Nigeria today, they count the creative arts among their top five foreign currency earners.

The potential for Nollywood to grow is yet to be fully explored. It has been touted as a model for Africa's development strategies because it originated, developed and was driven by ordinary people without external expertise and resources, becoming an export industry and jobs creator (Ezeonu 2013). Sadly, across Africa, including Zimbabwe, strategies that do not originate in government planning or have been blessed by donors are not accepted. This marginalises young people, especially those who are not employed and are not educated. As the foregoing has shown, several factors that have marginalised young people in and through education: the academic biases which have created an elitist education system that ignores the vast majority; the gender biases that neglect female students' needs; poverty seen in the high number of OVCs with no assistance and at risk of dropping out; and relentless graduate unemployment.

Work and employment

As noted in the definition of marginalisation above, access to and forms of employment/wage work or income-earning activities determine inclusion or exclusion in the economy and polity (Leysens 2006). In Zimbabwe, unemployment in the formal sector has been a challenge since late 1980s (Herbst 1989). In 1991-1995 when economic structural adjustment policies were introduced, whole sections of the manufacturing sector buckled under competition from imports or closed due to other viability challenges such as lack of foreign currency, and shrinking local markets as inflation soared and buying power declined. The resultant de-industrialisation created job losses. Many people resorted to the informal sector and other forms of employment. However, wage work was always male biased because of the colonial legacy of biased labour markets, education policies and cultural practices that preferred women who resided in rural areas where they engaged in farming while men were wage workers in urban areas (Potts 2000). These biases have persisted, as indicated in Table 3 below.

Table 3: Male and female economic activities in Zimbabwe

Activity	Male	Female	Population
Paid work	67,1	32,9	1,282,489
Employer	62,1	37,9	16,570
Own account agriculture	41,8	58,2	2,918,762
Own account other	57,1	42,9	829,458
Unpaid family worker	51,9	48,1	193,285
Looking for work/ Unemployed	64,1	35,9	371,244
Total	**51,7**	**48,3**	**5,611,808**

Source: ZimStat (2017: 83)

As evinced in the statistics above, there are comparatively more men in all economic activities except in agriculture, which is the domain of women. Agriculture towers over other activities and yet most women do not own land autonomously. However, women lack access to resources as is shown below. It is important to note too that almost a million Zimbabweans are self-employed ('own account other'). Although they have income, own account production is susceptible to variations in earnings especially when activities are in the lower end of the informal sector and sensitive to wider socio-economic contexts such as on-going COVID-19 restrictions, hyperinflation, and harassment by the police.

Women's access to resources

Gender equality in access to resources has been a rallying call in feminist campaigns, as seen in the Convention on the Elimination of all forms of Discrimination against Women (CEDAW), the Beijing Platform for Action (BPfA), the SADC Protocol for Gender and Development, the MDGs, the SDGs and the 2013 constitution. Access to resources not only enables autonomous decision-making but also allows women and girls options to leave abusive relationships. The reason why women's economic performance is low compared to men has to do with biases in access to resources such as credit, information, educational achievements and land.

In terms of access to land, fewer women than men got land in reforms since the 1980s. Jacobs (1991: 21-2) argues that although land reform was supposed to be the main mechanism of redressing colonial injustices, gender imbalances were overlooked in its implementation. Land was given to adults over 20 years of age, married or widowed with dependents and not in wage work. However, prejudices visited on women in formal employment did not seem to count. Permits were given to men as heads of households with no redress for women in the event of divorce or widowhood. Goebel (2007) shows that life in resettlement areas became desperate in the 2000s on account of deteriorating economic conditions, and the HIV and AIDS scourge, which undermined the viability of farming activities. Despite these lessons, the fast track land reform of 2000 did not improve ordinary women's access to land. Moyo (2011: 504) notes that between 12% and 18% of women accessed land during fast track land reform; most were relatively affluent. Less well-off women faced prejudice when they applied for land. As a result, despite knowledge and evidence that women dominate in agriculture, and are less represented in paid work. very little was done to make land available to them. As noted by Win (2004), former President Robert Mugabe was against women getting land in their own right.

When it comes to credit, women have limited access for a range of reasons, including limited financial literacy, lack of collateral and not having bank accounts because they are not formally employed. Under Agenda 2030, financial inclusion is a major concern internationally. Governments are implored to collaborate with players in the business sector to ensure the realisation of all goals. In this respect, there are donor efforts to improve women's bankability and financial literacy. Other than the Women's Bank, the Alliance for Financial Inclusion (AFI 2019) says that there is a women's desk/unit in all banks to improve women's access to banking information, credit, and business opportunities.

A cursory analysis of data published by AFI (ibid.: 10) shows that financial inclusion is still a pipe dream for Zimbabwean women. Out of US$135 million made available by or through the RBZ for vulnerable and excluded groups (women, youth, and persons with disability), there are no women engaged in exporting and only two doing bankable horticultural projects (ibid.). The vast majority of women are borrowing money for cross-border trade, an activity in which about 33% of borrowers are men. Women are still lagging behind in accessing loans, without which their status, income generating activities and participation in the economy remain limited. This constrains the possibility to have savings and own property. Furthermore, bank currently exclude women if they do not have proof of regular income. Mobile banking is less rigorous in its requirements, and may be a viable option, but its activities are currently limited by RBZ directives. That said, researchers warn against transformation of gender relations based on economic activity as indicating feminist activism that has been hijacked by neoliberal thinking. This does not necessarily attend to changing gender relations in order to ensure social justice (Stuart and Woodroffe 2016).

Youth and employment

Young people are the worst affected when it comes to wage work. School leaver unemployment has been relentless since the late 1980s. Graduate unemployment is also relentless (Gukurume 2017). Young people resort to informal sector work, but it is not what they want; they do it as a stopgap measure. Although official statistics indicate that there are few people who are looking for work, sentiments of young people counted as doing own account production indicate that many would rather be in formal work than self-employed.

Table 4: Age and percentage of employment activity in 2017

Age range	Paid work	Em-ployer	Own account agriculture	Own account other	Unpaid family worker	Looking/ unem-ployed
15-19	3,8	2,8	10,1	2,7	40,8	16,1
20-24	12,6	2,4	12,5	12,1	33,8	32,5
25-29	17,0	11,2	10,4	17,7	13,9	17,5
30-34	16,8	8,7	11,8	20,5	3,3	11,0
35-39	15,5	14,6	10,1	14.9	3.9	9,3

Source: ZimStat (2017)

From the above table, it appears that for young people age is important for getting wage work; the older one is the better the chance, assuming that one has qualifications, while younger people are doing unpaid work for their relatives. Many young people are self-employed, in agriculture or other sectors. However, these forms of employment are sensitive to unpredictable weather patterns and/or high-handed policy responses such as pervasive harassment, disruptions, relocations and other forms of law enforcement under militarisation and because of patronage.

Most of the self-employment of young in the informal sector is seen as a nuisance, as subversive non-work that has become the centre of fights between the ruling party and the opposition to control urban populations (McGregor 2013). The conflict has seen young people co-opted as willing instruments of violence sent to take over market stalls and the council flats of rivals, and to subject members of the public to extortion. In the violence that ensues, not only are youth militias stigmatised for the terror they unleash, but livelihoods in the informal sector have become increasingly precarious.

Youth empowerment through financial inclusion is also a major consideration. However, statistics published by AFI (2019) show that there is a long way to go, as few young people are recipients of loans.. Meanwhile, the events seen at market stalls (McGregor 2013) show that access to loans is not a solution.

Political participation and decision-making

Political participation has been a major focus for feminist activists and gender advocates since the 1990s. It is about exercising citizenship rights and aspirations for equity and equality. In its ideal forms, it seeks transformation from male-dominated institutions in terms of staffing, policy-making, implementation and evaluation (Gouws 1996). The participation of women in politics and decision making ensures their visibility in the corridors of power, and there is a possibility of social change through emulation in lower-level institutions which has the potential to create role models for younger women (Britton 2002). Furthermore, feminist activists assume that when women are not making decisions that matter to their short- and long-term needs, transformation of gender relations is slow.

Consequently, international and regional protocols on gender such the BPfA and the SADC Protocol on Gender and Development recognise political participation and decision making as important arenas of social change. These organisations implore governments to take deliberate steps to ensure that women are not only represented but that there is gender parity at different levels of decision making. Furthermore, section 17 of the 2013 constitution stipulates that there should be equal representation of men and women in all sectors and at all levels. The implementation of these commitments and protocols, and well as compliance with the 2013 constitution, provides an insight into the marginalisation of women. Governments and political parties are expected to give progress reports to international and regional bodies in order to exert peer pressure to ensure that reforms are effected internationally.

Guidance for youth participation in decision-making is provided by the United Nations Convention on the Right of the Child (UNCRC), the African Union's African Youth Charter (AYC) of 2006 and in the 2013 Constitution of Zimbabwe. Zimbabwe is party to the UNCRC and AYC. UNCRC's Article 12 says children have a right to be heard and to have appropriate representation; Articles 13 to 15 enunciate other rights such as access to information, and freedom of thought and association. The AYC's preamble clearly refers to poverty, unemployment, public health challenges, gender-based violence (GBV) and discrimination as forms of social exclusion visited on young people that should be eliminated. It lists a bill of rights that young people must enjoy such as freedom of expression and association, the right to privacy, to all dimensions of development and access to information. Its Article 11 specifically addresses youth participation and says that states should 'guarantee' youth participation in parliament, and in decision making at all levels of society, including in civic organisations. Article 12 states that youth concerns should be mainstreamed across all sectors in national development planning, be debated in parliament and be included in budgetary allocations. Section 20 of the 2013 Constitution reiterates the AYC's provisions, namely that the state has to ensure that youths have access to appropriate education and training, and to recreational activities, and are protected from harmful cultural practices, exploitation and all forms of abuse. Furthermore, it states that such measures and programmes should be inclusive, non-partisan and national in character.

Women's participation in politics and decision-making since independence

Since independence, women have occupied less than 20% of parliamentary seats in any election. Even at independence, when women combatants were recently demobilised, when refugees and exiles had returned, when the ideology or propaganda of the war was fresh in people's mind and when there was talk of social transformation, only a handful of women were voted into office. These women were mostly wives of political elites in the nationalist movements (Nhongo-Simbanegavi 2000). From this small group of women (see Table 5 below) the first female cabinet ministers were selected.

As Josefsson (2014) and Goetz (2002) have noted, male leaders maintain control of the party by choosing women they trust with their vision, the party agenda, and who will vote with the party and will not challenge party interests in parliamentary debates. They choose the wives, widows or children of their comrades to capitalise on multiple loyalties and kinship, or clients whose obedience is rewarded through other means. Feminists and gender activists whose interests lie with changing gender relations for ordinary women fare poorly under these conditions. They are distrusted and seen as subversive. A good example is that of Margaret Dongo, who despite her 'struggle credentials' (Parpart 2015) was deselected in the 1995 elections because she challenged male political elites (Maphosa et al. 2015).

Beyond the experiences of specific female politicians, one can also refer to the former President Mugabe's posturing on women, which blew hot and cold. While he seemed to support women's political participation, he also rebuked feminism and quests for gender equality on several occasions as anti-family and anti-culture. This perhaps shows that politicians feel the need to comply with donor pressure, to present a good image as reformers but also to assure local patriarchal interests that nothing will change. Women's quests for political representation therefore fall between the cracks in these contradictions.

The few women who become MPs do not seem to be able to ensure substantive representation of women's strategic gender needs (Josefsson 2014). This is due in part to the fact that often there is a 'party line' to be followed in debates in parliament. When the party line does not include women's strategic gender needs or when leaders of parties can, without consultation, make pronouncements that cannot be challenged and which become policy, then women MPs are easily gagged. A good example is the land reform process. Women were clamouring to access land in their own right until ex-President Mugabe, as quoted by Win (2004: 18), proclaimed that, 'If women want land in their own right, they should never get married'.

The clamour ebbed without debate as the President's personal opinion became de facto practice. Land reform continued with married men as the leading beneficiaries. In another example, cited by Christiansen (2009), the former President warned women not to be persuaded by foreign influences regarding rights. This ambivalence to women's rights seems to also send a message that this is not priority. The president's statements were not debated in parliament, the party or cabinet. If activists could not influence him then the gender equality cause remained on the balance.

In spite of being party to several protocols that seek change in women's political participation such as CEDAW, the BPfA in 1995 and SADC Protocol on Gender and Development of 2005 and 2008 as well as Millennium Development Goals (MDGs), Zimbabwe did comparatively little to ensure gender equality in representation in higher offices in the period under analysis.

Table 5: The number and percentage of female parliamentarians since 1980

Election	No. of female MPs	Percentage
1980	9 (out of 100)	9
1985	8 (out of 100)	8
1990	17 (out of 150)	11.3
1995	21 (out of 150)	14
2000	14 (out of 150)	9.3
2005	24 (out of 150)	16

Election	No. of female MPs	Percentage
2008	30 (out of 210)	14.29
2013		31
2018		34

Note: In 2013 elections 26 women were elected and 60 became MPs through reserved seats.

Sources: https://www.parlzim.gov.zw/about-parliament/publications/history-of-women-parlamentarians (accessed 5 Sept 2020) EISA African Democracy Encyclopaedia Project https://www.eisa.org/wep/zim2008women2.htm (accessed 8 October 2020), UN Women (2013), Butaumocho (2018) and Maphosa et al. (2015).

In 2005, SADC implored member states to have 30% female representation. By 2008 they were calling for 50:50 representation. It was only in the 2013 elections that reservations earned women 40% representation in parliament (UN Women 2013). However, the quota system and reservation of seats have not been sustained in subsequent elections, despite Section 17 of the 2013 Constitution stipulating that the state has a duty to ensure equal representation. During the run-up to the 2018 elections, women lobbied President Mnangagwa to continue with the system of reservations, but to no avail. Instead, militarisation was in evidence. Thus, neither calls for quotas and affirmative action in regional protocols and international agreements nor constitutional provisions give assurances for gender equality. To be effective, these instruments depend on the goodwill and cooperation of male leaders of parties to sustain numerical representation of women at 50:50. Meanwhile, male leaders of the parties have other political interests to attend to which compete with and against women's calls for equality.

Other reasons for this history of comparatively poor representation can be gleaned from former president Mugabe's speeches in which he persistently rationalised that there were no qualified women that he could have on his line-up of candidates (Maphosa et al. 2015). By 'qualifications' he was not obviously referring to leadership, or literacy, but to a good fit with his party's political vision, objectives and strategies. Among other qualifications that the ruling party looks for are 'struggle credentials' (Parpart 2015) or links to men with struggle credentials to ensure loyalty and trustworthiness.

Clearly, male leaders do not see proficiency in gender transformation and advocacy as a worthy qualification. If they did, they would have seen the technical expertise in the women's movement. Furthermore, unlike in South Africa, in Zimbabwe the links and collaborations between political parties and the women's movement have been fraught with distrust and mutual suspicion since independence (Nhongo-Simbanegavi 2000; Essof 2012). As long as the women's movement relies on donor funds, it is seen as open to foreign influences which in moments of crises (and there have been many) are viewed as anti-government and therefore not worth listening to.

The role of patriarchal cultural norms

Patriarchal cultural norms are deeply ingrained in the Zimbabwean psyche. They pervade the courts of law, parliament, traditional courts, the media and other institutions. Women, who are vocal, who ask questions and demand that men be held to account, risk verbal abuse, name-calling and heckling in public including in official gatherings. The media seems to have no scruples in publicising these events, thus re-traumatising victims and warning other women not to follow suit. Thus, to be a female leader one has to withstand public scrutiny of one's private life, and current and past relationships. It is worse for single women. Irrespective of their professional standing, women are subject to episodic or constant verbal abuse when in public office whenever their actions are deemed to be against the interests of sections of society.

Current MPs such as Ms Priscilla Misihairambi-Mushonga live with heckling almost daily in their parliamentary work as long as they stand up to male peers, show support for female peers or bring up issues of concern to women's strategic gender needs. It has been argued that the experiences of female candidates and senior members of the election agency occupy a 'toxic terrain'.[1] This discourages women, including experienced politicians, from running for office again. Furthermore, it fuels the antipathy that feminists have for party politics (Goetz 2002). Where there are weak links between the women's movements and political parties, women's representation falls through the cracks. The enduring effects are that women continue to be excluded from decision making.

In courts of law women's rights can be clawed back, as seen in the controversial Magaya vs Magaya case in 1999 in which the courts argued that daughters could not inherit ahead of sons irrespective of objective criteria such as birth order (the notion of primogeniture or ultimogeniture).

---

1   'Political terrain toxic for women', *Business Times*, 2 July 2020.

The infamy of this case attracted international protests, but the courts did not change, arguing for justification in terms of Zimbabwe's customary laws (Bigge and von Briesen 2000). The logic of customary laws and inheritance cannot be explained here due to limitations of space, save to say that citing patrilineal kinship norms, customary laws emphasise inheritance within the lineage. Because women are expected to move to their husbands' families or place of residence on marriage, they are seen as transient members in their families of birth but remain strangers in their husbands' families. Therefore, women as daughters or wives are denied inheritance in either kin affiliation. To keep wealth in the family, men inherit because their lineage membership is seen as stable.

Prompted in part by the escalation of HIV and AIDS, in the late 1990s parliament passed the Traditional Leaders' Act in a bid to conserve African traditions which were seen as a solution to the scourge when public health experts said a human rights approach was best (Ranchod-Nilsson 2006). The cultural norms that perpetuated inequalities and hierarchies in socio-sexual relations and fuelled women and youth's vulnerability to infection were disregarded.

Another illustration of biases in parliament is seen in debates about the Domestic Violence bill in 2007. A male opposition MP suggested that the bill was against men's prerogatives to control their wives after paying bride-wealth. He also said that women should conduct themselves appropriately by not dressing in an inviting (sic) manner, and that women leaders should be married. These sentiments seemed to resonate with other men according to extensive media coverage at the time (Christiansen 2009: 183-5). Men who opposed the bill argued that equality between men and women is antithetical to African culture and dismissed the bill as Eurocentric. Feminist activists had to counter that they are patriotic Zimbabweans, concerned about the rights of survivors of violence and want peace in families. It seems that some people abhor change entailed in gender equality arguing that such change corrupts 'culture'. The reality that culture is dynamic is lost in these emotional arguments. In any case, the colonial legacy and its corruption of African ways of life that are encapsulated in notions of 'African culture' is not dealt with.

In traditional courts, chiefs across Matabeleland were protesting the installation of a female chief in 1996 arguing that it was unprecedented and therefore a corruption of Ndebele culture (Lindgren 2005). The incoming chief was the then single and eldest daughter of the deceased chief who had no biological sons. These few examples show that patriarchal norms pervade all institutions, including the courts – which should be even-handed, interpret the law and not decode culture.

Cabinet and other high posts held by women

Cabinet posts held by women have focussed on 'soft issues' such as women's affairs, youth affairs, small-scale enterprises and social welfare, portfolios which also tend to have limited budgets. To date, no women have been appointed to ministries of finance, industrialisation or higher education. In 2005 to 2014, when Dr Joyce Mujuru held the position of Vice President, she did not finish her term as she fell victim to intra-party jostling for power and positions in anticipation of 2018 elections. After the military take-over in November 2017, the first woman to head the all-powerful Ministry of Defence was appointed in the person of Ms Oppah Muchinguri-Kashiri. During her tenure, the military unleashed unprecedented violence on ordinary people. She has not commented on the violence. This shows that when women preside over such androcentric institutions and when there is a party line to be followed, the appointments do not lead to a change in institutional practices and cultures.

Women are, however, making inroads in the judiciary. Three out of seven constitutional court judges are women. Women are judges and magistrates in lower courts as well as working as prosecutors, but with the 'politicisation' of the judiciary, intimidation, 'malleable reports', threats and enticement of technical staff in the court system (Verheul 2013: 773-7), especially after 2000, the high number of women in judiciary services is not transformative. The appointment of women in this instance has not led to changes in how ordinary citizens experience state power and state-society relations.

Youth and political participation

The AYC's enforceability is weakened by dynamics within the African Union (AU) which avowedly eschews interference in member states' affairs. Consequently, even when the constitution of Zimbabwe reiterates issues and concerns raised in international agreements, implementation is lax and seems optional when it should not be. Therefore, even when it is clear that Zimbabwe has not complied, as is explained below, the non-compliance is not dealt with by African peers who seem to have similar or worse problems.

The UNCRC's active monitoring by UN agencies such as UNICEF, as well as the donor resources they wield, ensures that aspects of participation are implemented such as through junior parliaments and councils. However, they are ritualistic and tokenistic. These institutions are there to illustrate compliance with international conventions rather than for transformation of social relations by changing age inequalities and hierarchies in decision making. Furthermore, it is not clear how young people who speak at these events decide on the issues they discuss, and whether or not the speeches originate from the young speakers themselves, or are edited by adults. Evidence of gerontocratic relations in schools suggest that teachers and parents probably act as gatekeepers to maintain respectability by preventing discussion of issues that would embarrass political elites.

Despite these weaknesses, young people's participation is included in reports to UN organs that monitor compliance with international conventions, as noted by the Global Youth Coalition on HIV/AIDS (GYCA)'s shadow report on Zimbabwe to the UN General Assembly Special Session in 2008. Such forms of participation are good for public relations but do little to ensure that young people's voices are heard, or their aspirations attended to. GYCA (2008) reiterates this point by arguing that policies for and on youth sexuality and the prevention of HIV/AIDS leave a lot to be desired as the government persists on abstinence-only sexuality education; the ministry of education resists the distribution of condoms in schools; youth participation is not stressed in the national youth policy; young people do not contribute to making policies that affect them; and a lack of resources and the paucity of age disaggregated data in all sectors impede the mainstreaming of youth concerns.

When young people below 40 years of age were elected to parliament in the past, they acted more as activists of their parties and did not speak for the plight of young people in general. One such young person, Joanah Mamombe (37 years old in 2020), an MDC MP, has been subjected to unprecedented abuse, detention, harassment and a delayed trial. Thus, young people not only lack substantive representation in parliament, in local government and at community level, but politics has been presented as a threatening area of life. When youth participation is implemented with donor support, such efforts fizzle out once donor support ends (Fanelli et al. 2007).

Youth and rhizomatic politics

As excluded as they are, young people increasingly resort to what Castells (2012) describes as 'rhizomatic politics', in which power and resistance are expressed and wielded underground, enabled by the internet. It also refers to language that adults ignore as 'child's play' but which becomes a code for political aspirations and is used to communicate resistance. Sometimes it entails the adaptation of emoticons used widely in social media. Rhizomatic politics have allowed young people to express themselves by calling local leaders and the international community to account for their continued marginalisation in the economy and in society in general. Social media allow rapid and multiple sharing and the spread is uncontrollable once the message is out.

Some researchers argue that through social media, ordinary citizens have reclaimed their freedom of expression, found a voice, and can contest the narratives of political elites (Mavhunga 2009: 160). Social media have also allowed activists and professionals to create alternative platforms to share information about what is happening in Zimbabwe through online newspapers and radio stations based outside the country. However, state security agencies have since acquired technology to jam some of the broadcasts (ibid.: 164), and use malware to target individuals or their organisations to steal personal information.

Researchers note that political activism using social media is increasingly a double-edged sword, because it allows investigators to intercept communications unseen. Notwithstanding end-to-end encryption and other security technologies, many activists' digital footprints, locations and other identifiers are traceable, thus diminishing advantages of rhizomatic activities. Recorded material provides evidence which officials can use against young activists.

Furthermore, reliance on social media does not allow the formation of strong social connections, as it privileges virtual bonds that are amenable to manipulation by state agents, criminals and others. This 'deformed sociality' (Giroux 2015) also undermines political activity and shows that politics through social media is malleable, making it difficult for people to discern whether a post is genuine or fake. There are indeed many websites for fact-checking, but perhaps only a few astute activists use them. The fear of ubiquitous and instantaneous surveillance leads to self-censorship, self-restraint and a distrust of others (McGregor 2013).

The following examples in the first half of 2020 speak to the ubiquity of surveillance and its danger:

- the rapid spread of the #ZimbabweanLivesMatter and suspicion that young activists and members of the opposition were behind it;
- the arrest and trial of the originator of #ThisFlag and activists using #ThisGown (Gukurume 2017);
- the abduction and torture of the lead satirist, a young woman, who parodies trending social events and their instigators under the banner of BusStop.tv;
- online micro-bloggers being rounded up for expressing views considered subversive;
- the abduction and torture of a young spokesperson of an association of medical students;
- student associations that sued education authorities over the hasty and unilateral roll-out of online learning in response to COVID-19 are yet to hear the outcome of their case.

Young people's political activity through social media is what Castells (2012) describes as 'networks of outrage' at the poverty, injustice, corruption, and lack of services visited on their lives. He argues that through sharing and exposing these multi-layered exclusions, young people hope for a resolution, hence the 'networks of outrage' are also 'networks of hope'.

In some cases, live coverage of arrests beamed through social media platforms has helped to alert the whole world to what is happening. However, those in power do not see these activities and cyber institutions in the same light. Indeed, the government even attempted to subpoena records of a private phone company for six months in 2020, arguing that some individuals were subverting the economy using mobile money transactions.2 If the search warrant had been granted, it would have given the government a stifling control over freedom of expression, association and movement. It would have instilled terror in people by demonstrating that there was nowhere to hide. Fortunately, the courts turned it down on grounds of privacy violation.

The expression of outrage is seen as subversive, while hopes of change

---

2 'Zimbabwe court suspends police search warrant against Econet', *Reuters*, 22 July 2020.

through speaking truth to power are reduced to treasonous aspirations for regime change. Outrage related to abductions and violations in the first half of 2020 spawned #ZimbabweanLivesMatter, which saw media, entertainment personalities, international football stars and well as several ex-presidents in the region using the hash tag and demanding that the authorities be sensitive to the plight of ordinary Zimbabweans. Although government officials denied the allegations, the power of exposure through social media cannot be underestimated. However, social media use does not result in changes in representation or discussion of youth concerns in parliament. Furthermore, rhizomatic politics are typically amenable to invisibility and secrecy because of risks. Thus, the activists cannot convert successes online into votes in the ballot box when elections take place.

Political participation: for what and on whose terms?

There are forms of participation that the ruling party tolerates. These include an appreciation of the liberation struggle, and the celebration of heroes/heroines of the struggle through the introduction of NASS in 2000. These changes went hand in with the introduction of the National Youth Service (NYS) which sought to indoctrinate 'born-frees' into the ideologies of the liberation struggle and subservience to the ruling party. NYS attendees were promised preferential access to entry-level work and places in vocational and technical colleges. In a study of local politics, McGregor (2013: 786-7) shows that NYS graduates became a de facto, albeit invisible, authority that responded to political elites in the ruling party but whose existence the elites denied and dissociated themselves from. They organised themselves into shadowy groups used for surveillance, to attack dissenters and members of the opposition, to harrass members of the public, to run markets and control access to stalls in contravention of council bye-laws, and to gain control over council flats by forcibly evicting occupants. Young people who participated in this violence became rich and were inserted into patronage networks, further marginalising their peers who had no powerful patrons or political networks. Many non-partisan young people live in terror because of these militias. Those who could leave low-income areas did. Incidents of harassment go unreported for fear of escalating abuse.

By contrast, some young people within the opposition ran for council elections after 2008 because adults were afraid of violence from the ruling party militias. However, because of limited education, and a lack of houses and other services, these councillors are corruptible (ibid.: 789). Because the ministry responsible for local government is controlled by the ruling party, officials with long experience routinely try to compromise the councillors, tempting them with housing plots, market stalls and other kickbacks (ibid.: 790). Some councillors and their constituents feel that to counter their chronic exclusion they should create their own patronage networks. It can be concluded that chronic exclusion leaves politicians and activists morally fragile even when they are in office.

The foregoing discussion shows that there are no policies that demonstrate an appreciation of the need for youth inclusion and the deleterious effects of exclusion. Even where there are young councillors, their presence has not been leveraged to tackle substantive issues affecting the youth. As a result, there are no skills training centres, credit schemes or banking facilities, contrary to AFI (2019) claims of efforts to promote the financial inclusion of marginalised groups.

Discussion and conclusion

The marginalisation of women and young people is due to a number of intertwined factors, including institutional issues, cultural beliefs and policy blind spots borne of limited or narrow understanding of generational and gender relations.

Institutionally, the ruling party claims that it delivered human rights to the nation and has a monopoly on ensuring gender equality and speaking for women. Furthermore, the party alone defines and defends the sovereignty of the nation (Nhongo-Simbanegavi 2000). With such powers, it overrides the constitution, the courts and national laws. It complies with international laws only selectively. As a result, because gender equality and youth empowerment are defined in a manner that suits the party, few argue. However, the results do not match aspirations of non-partisan citizens.

These processes reinforce traditions of gerontocracy and patriarchy, and keep women and youths out of power. Feminist and gender activists' antipathy to party politics, and political elites' suspicion of activists do not help. Excluded youth are easily used as pawns, as instruments of violence. The youth comply as a show of allegiance to political parties and political elites in the hope of carving out livelihoods of their own. Meanwhile, young people who are not affiliated to parties resort to rhizomatic politics on the Internet. The impact of such activities has yet to translate to votes.

The quantitative bias of education, to the exclusion of quality, has contributed to marginalisation. More graduates and school leavers are chasing a declining number of jobs as the economy shrinks. Policy makers focus on expanding university education, at the expense those without education, who experience worsening social exclusion. As unemployed young people resort to the informal sector, harassment and hastily implemented relocations worsen exclusion. Social exclusion is perpetuated by policymaking and implementation, institutional structure and values, and cultural beliefs such as gerontocracy and patriarchy. As noted in the Introduction, although some argue that exclusion can lead to revolts, others argue that the excluded are too preoccupied with survival to revolt.

References

Abraham, R. (2003) 'The localization of the O Level Art Examinations in Zimbabwe', *Studies in Art Education*, 45(1), pp. 73-87.

Alliance for Financial Inclusion (AFI) (2019) 'Gender, women's economic empowerment and financial inclusion in Zimbabwe'. Kuala Lumpur: AFI.

Barnes, T. (2007) '"History has to Play its Role": Constructions of Race and Reconciliation in Secondary School Historiography in Zimbabwe, 1980-2002', *Journal of Southern African Studies*, 33(3), pp. 633-651.

Bennell, P. and M. Ncube (1994) 'A University for the Povo? The Socio-economic Background of African University Students in Zimbabwe Since Independence', *Journal of Southern African Studies*, 20(4), pp. 587-601.

Bigge, D.M. and A. von Briesen (2000) 'Conflict in Zimbabwean Courts: Women's Rights and Indigenous Self-determination in *Magaya v Magaya*', *Harvard Human Rights Journal*, 13, pp. 289-313.

Boon, B. and J. Farnsworth (2011) 'Social Exclusion and Poverty: Translating Social Capital into Accessible Resources', *Social Policy & Administration*, 45(5), pp. 507-524.

Britton, H. (2002) 'Coalition Building, Election Rules, and Party Politics: South African Women's Path to Parliament', *Africa Today,* 49(4), pp. 33-67.

Castells, M. (2012) *Networks of outrage and hope – social movements in the Internet age*. Chichester: Wiley.

Christiansen, L.B. (2009) '"In our culture": How Debates about Zimbabwe's

Domestic Violence Law Became a "Culture Struggle"', *NORA - Nordic Journal of Feminist and Gender Research*, 17(3), pp. 175-191.

Dansereau, S. (2000) 'State, Capital and Labour: Veins, Fissures and Faults in Zimbabwe's Mining Sector', *Labour, Capital and Society*, 33(2), pp. 216-254.

Essof, S. (2013) *SheMurenga: The Zimbabwe Women's Movement 1995-2000*. Harare: Weaver Press.

Ezeonu, I. (2013) 'Nollywood Consensus: Modeling a Development Pathway for Africa', *The Global South*, 7(1), pp. 179-199.

Fanelli, C.W., R. Musarandega and L. Chawanda (2007) 'Child Participation in Zimbabwe's National Action for Orphans and Other Vulnerable Children: Progress, Challenges and Possibilities', *Children, Youth and Environments*, 17(3), pp. 122-145.

Giroux, H.A. (2015) 'Selfie Culture in the Age of Corporate and State Surveillance', *Third Text*, 29(3), pp. 155-164.

Global Youth Coalition on HIV/AIDS (GYCA) (2008) '2008 National Youth Shadow Report: Zimbabwe'. New York and Accra: GYCA.

Goebel, A. (2007) '"We Are Working for Nothing": Livelihoods and Gender Relations in Rural Zimbabwe, 2000-06', *Canadian Journal of African Studies*, 41(2), pp. 226-257.

Goetz, A.M. (2002) 'No Shortcuts to Power: Constraints on Women's Political Effectiveness in Uganda', *Journal of Modern Africa Studies*, 40(4), pp. 549-575.

Gouws, A. (1996) 'The rise of the Femocrat?', *Agenda*, 12(30), pp. 31-43.

Government of Zimbabwe (GoZ) (2019) '2018 Primary and secondary education statistics report'. Harare: Ministry of Primary and Secondary Education.

Grant, M. (2003) '"Difficult debut": Social and Economic Identities of Urban Youth in Bulawayo, Zimbabwe', *Canadian Journal of African Studies*, 37(2-3), pp. 411-439.

Gukurume, S. (2017) '#ThisFlag and #ThisGown Cyber Protests in Zimbabwe: Reclaiming Political Space', *African Journalism Studies*, 38(2), pp. 49-70.

Herbst, J. (1989) 'Political impediments to economic rationality: explaining

Zimbabwe's failure to reform its public sector', *The Journal of Modern African Studies*, 27(1), pp. 67-84.

Jacobs, S. (1991) 'Land Resettlement and Gender in Zimbabwe', *The Journal of Modern African Studies*, 29(3), pp. 521-528.

Johnson, D.F. (1990) 'The politics of literacy and schooling in Zimbabwe', *Review of African Political Economy*, 17(48), pp. 99-106.

Jones, J.L. (2010) '"Nothing is Straight in Zimbabwe": The Rise of the Kukiya-kiya Economy 2000-2008', *Journal of Southern African Studies*, 26(2), pp. 285-299.

Josefsson, C. (2014) 'Who benefits from gender quotas? Assessing the impact of election procedure reform on Members of Parliament's attributes in Uganda', *International Political Science Review*, 35(1), pp. 93-105.

Kamete, A.Y (2008) 'Planning versus youth: Stamping out spatial unruliness in Harare', *Geoforum*, 39(5), pp. 1721-1733.

Leysens, A.J. (2006) 'Social forces in Southern Africa: transformation from below?' *The Journal of Modern African Studies*, 44(1), pp. 31-58.

Lindgren, B. (2005) 'The Politics of Ethnicity as an Extended Case: Thoughts on a Chiefly Succession Crisis', *Social Analysis: The International Journal of Anthropology*, 49(3), pp. 234-253.

MacKenzie, C.G. (1988) 'Zimbabwe's educational miracle and the problems it has created', *International Review of Education,* 34(3), pp. 337-353.

Maphosa, M., N. Tshuma and G. Maviza (2015) 'Participation of Women in Zimbabwean Politics and the Mirage of Gender Equity', *Ubuntu: Journal of Conflict and Social Transformation*, 4(2), pp. 127-159.

Matereke, K.P. (2012) '"Whipping Them into Line": The Dual Crisis of Education and Citizenship in Postcolonial Zimbabwe', *Educational Philosophy and Theory*, 44(2), pp. 84-100.

Mavhunga, C. (2009) 'The glass fortress: Zimbabwe's cyber-guerrilla warfare', *Journal of International Affairs*, 62(2), pp. 159-173

McGregor, J. (2013) 'Surveillance and the City: Patronage, Power-sharing and the Politics of Urban Control in Zimbabwe', *Journal of Southern African Studies*, 39(4), pp. 783-805.

Moyo, S. (2011) 'Three decades of agrarian reforms in Zimbabwe', *The*

Journal of Peasant Studies, 38(3), pp. 493-531.

Nhongo-Simbanegavi, J. (2000) *For Better or Worse? Women and ZANLA in Zimbabwe's Liberation Struggle*. Harare: Weaver Press.

Nyazema, N. (2010) 'The Zimbabwe Crisis and the Provision of Social Services', *Journal of Developing Societies*, 26(2), pp. 233-261

Pape, J. (1998) 'Changing Education for Majority Rule in Zimbabwe and South Africa', *Comparative Education Review*, 42(3), pp. 253-266.

Parpart, J.L. (2015) 'Militarised masculinities, heroes and gender inequality during and after the nationalist struggle in Zimbabwe', *NORMA: International Journal for Masculinity Studies*, 10(3-4), pp. 312-325.

Potts, D. (2000) 'Worker-peasants and Farmer-housewives in Africa: The Debate about "Committed" Farmers, Access to Land and Agricultural Production', *Journal of Southern African Studies*, 26(4), pp. 807-832.

Ranchod-Nilsson, S. (2006) 'Gender Politics and the Pendulum of Political and Social Transformation in Zimbabwe', *Journal of Southern African Studies*, 32(1), pp. 46-69.

Stuart, E. and J. Woodroffe (2016) 'Leaving no-one behind: Can the Sustainable Development Goals succeed where the Millennium Development Goals lacked?' *Gender & Development*, 24(1), pp. 69–81.

Training and Research Support Centre (TARSC) (2012) 'Tracking the Governance and Accountability of the Basic Education And Assistance Module in Ten Districts of Zimbabwe'. Harare: TARSC.

Verheul. S. (2013) '"Rebels" and "Good boys": Patronage, Intimidation and Resistance in Zimbabwe's Attorney General's Office after 2000', *Journal of Southern Africa Studies*, 39(4), pp. 765-782.

Win, E. (2004) '"Are there any people here?": Violence against women in the Zimbabwean conflict', *Agenda*, 18(59), pp. 17-21.

Zimbabwe National Statistics Agency (ZimStat) (2017) 'Inter-Censal Demographic Survey 2017'. Harare: ZimStat.

―――― (2018) 'Education Report 2017'. Harare: ZimStat.

Zvobgo, R. (1987) 'Education and the Challenge of Independence', in I. Mandaza (ed.) *Zimbabwe: The Political Economy of Transition, 1980-1986*. Dakar: Codesria.

Media sources

Butaumocho, Ruth (2018) 'Election 2018: women fail to grain ground' https://www.herald.co.zw/election-2018-women-fail-to-gain-ground/

UN Women (2013) 'Women make up more than one-third of Zimbabwe's new parliament' https://www.unwomen.org/en/news/stories/2013/9/zimbabwe-women-mps-sworn-in

8

Conclusion

David Kaulemu and Lloyd Sachikonye

The period between 1980 and 2020 has seen Zimbabwe and Zimbabweans move from being admired regionally and globally as liberation heroes with great potential for exemplary development to being a basket case. Contributions in this volume grapple with the reasons why. They describe and assess this forty-year national journey with a view to encouraging Zimbabweans to reflect on important national issues so that the next forty years may be better years for every citizen. The spirit of the contributors is characterised by an unquestionable commitment to Zimbabwe as a nation and yet imbued with a certain sense of disappointment that it could have done much better than it has done so far. This however is not the end of the story.

Chapters in this volume analyse in order to find a way forward. They avoid, in the words of Pope Francis (2015), 'an excess of diagnosis, which at times leads us to multiply words and to revel in pessimism and negativity'. None of the chapters are pessimistic, nor are they negative about the country. They are realistic about the gravity of the historical moment the nation faces and the high moral, political and economic mountains we must climb before we can see the Promised Land. Yet they are full of hope, as they are convinced that we have not come to the end of history. One thing that comes out clearly in all the chapters, is the human agency that has brought us to where we are. The analyses show how our predicament is neither natural nor inevitable. This gives us hope. As Zygmunt Bauman explains (in Giddens 1991: 12),

Once we understand better how the apparently natural, inevitable, eternal aspects of our lives have been brought into being through the exercise of human power and human resources, we will find it hard to accept once more that they are immune and impenetrable to human action.

This is good news, as it gives us hope that the politics of 'resilient authoritarianism', the patriarchal cultures that support the exclusion of the youth and women from development processes and the economic management styles that have turned Zimbabweans into economic migrants and refugees are all not natural and inevitable. As pointed out in the Introduction, analysts disagree on why the 'processes of development and democratisation have proved more protracted and formidable than originally anticipated'. This is not surprising, as these questions are political and ethical. Social sciences 'cannot break off completely from their insider's knowledge of the experience they try to comprehend' (Bauman in Giddens 1991: 9). Ha-Joon Chang (2014: 401) has helped us to appreciate how economic theories and policies are 'political arguments'.

Recap of the chapters and salient issues

Chigumira and Kwaramba draw out the various ethical arguments in assessing the Fast Track Land Reform Programme; Sachikonye unpacks the ethical and political arguments surrounding the development-governance nexus; and Mapope interrogates the politics of foreign aid. From this perspective, contributions in this volume return to the 'political economy' approach, which tries to bring out the value judgments behind economic theories and social policies. David Kaulemu calls for the widening of the national social imaginary in order to encourage more inclusive narratives that build national confidence without shying away from robust self-criticism. The implications of narrow national narratives are seen in the way the Zimbabwean community has restricted success in national dialogues, engagements and debates resulting in conflicts and the exclusion of many Zimbabweans including civil society, churches and non-governmental organisations from national dialogue processes. All inclusive national dialogues, supported by national and global solidarity can be the best foundation for the future growth and development of the country.

Lloyd Sachikonye offers a deeper analysis of the reasons for lack of success in national development and governance. The political nature of this question and the ethical assumptions behind each position are clearly explained. Some analysts focus on the autocratic political leadership style of ZANU-PF. Others blame it on the systemic failure of the post-colonial government. Government analysts blame the sanctions applied against the Mugabe administration by the West from 2002. The chapters in the volume admit that these different perspectives and assessments have some truth in them. From the narrowness of the social imaginary, comes the 'concentration rather than dispersal of power' in the party-state.

For many of the chapters, it is this 'resilient authoritarianism' that has stood in the way of many potential development processes and marred initiatives that could have brought about genuine social transformation. Sachikonye demonstrates how the political governance issues have undermined accountability resulting in 'unchecked corruption and significant misappropriation of public resources'.

Poor political governance and conflicts have stalled development, resulting in much suffering. Many Zimbabweans have used migration as a response to this suffering and as a way of improving their prospects for survival and realising their professional potential outside the country. Chilunjika and Masiiwa explore how economic management is linked to trade and migration policies. Describing how deindustrialisation, unemployment, informalisation of industry and poor policies have caused a lot of suffering, they also identify opportunities for future development emanating from trade, investment and migration. They point to lessons from other countries and how those countries have benefited from the participation of diaspora investments through remittance flows. For a country that suffered UN sanctions as Rhodesia, and targeted sanctions as Zimbabwe, migration must be seen as an opportunity for widening ideas, experiences, traditions, social networks and income for dealing with local challenges.

Rekopantswe Mate looks at the marginalisation of the youth and women in Zimbabwe's development. She dissects the forms of marginalisation that span from exclusion in schools and employment to marginalisation in social and political realms. She points out how feminist activists have focused on political participation as a means for expanding women's 'citizenship rights and aspirations for equity and equality'. The assumption is that the participation of women in politics and decision making ensures the opening up of more doors for more women and girls. She interrogates the patriarchal cultural norms ingrained in Zimbabwean institutions such as 'the courts of law, parliament, traditional courts and the media'. She engages with the question of excluded youth, who are used in political contestations as pawns and sometimes as instruments of violence for the ruling party and for opposition parties, and describes how non-political-party-affiliated young people resort to 'rhizomatic politics' on social media to fight for inclusivity. This chapter, as do other chapters in this collection, demonstrates how the political challenges that Zimbabweans face are more than party-political challenges. In many ways, they demonstrate how party politics has been restricting Zimbabwe's development potential.

George Mapope discusses the ethics and politics of foreign aid and social policy and assessed the role of aid in Zimbabwe's development. He helps us appreciate how aid has been used in the past and assesses how it could be used in future. He argues that foreign aid 'is central to explaining the trajectory of the economy and social policies, particularly those pertaining to poverty reduction'. The predominant forms of such foreign assistance, and the degree to which it has contributed to the development process are explored. In considering how aid has been both positive and negative, Mapope discusses the political role that it has played – from contributing to dependency, to being used as a political weapon for regime change 'to which the ZANU-PF government responded with a radical form of authoritarianism' and therefore worsened the crisis in the country. Zimbabwe must find a balanced role for foreign aid in the future.

Chigumira and Kwaramba analyse Zimbabwe's development from a political ecology perspective. They assess how different sectors of society and the economy have responded to uneven development in the enclave economic set up since independence (Kanyenze et al. 2011), and examine the political contestations that led to the implementation of the Fast Trask Land Reform Programme (FTLRP), illustrating the deep divisions and contrasting moral and political assumptions made by different sectors of the population. Following Moyo and Yeros (2005), Chigumira and Kwaramba argue for the conscientisation of Zimbabwean individuals and communities to facilitate meaningful participation in national government initiatives and decision making processes. They view the FTLRP as contributing to the democratisation process essential for Zimbabwe's growth and development, and as a process that helps to deracialise and build more inclusive spaces in the former large-scale commercial farms.

Reflections from the COVID-19 experience

As we celebrated our forty years of independence, the coronavirus hit the world and Zimbabwe was not spared. The virus exposed further the weaknesses of our development trajectory both nationally and globally. We can use this as an opportunity to reflect more deeply on the governance and policy directions we have taken and how we will need to adjust how we, as a nation, want to live together and to fit into the global systems. As some of the chapters in this volume demonstrate, the post-COVID-19 era demands a new vision of global, regional and national moral order – a new social imaginary that makes different assumptions and aspires to a cosmopolitan ideal that brings together people from different histories and backgrounds and cultivates healthier national and global citizenship. COVID-19 has shown how we now live in a globalised and 'risk society' (Giddens 1991: 3) in which national issues of human rights, land reform, climate change and personal health are no longer merely local issues. National sovereignties are now 'perforated sovereignties' (de Rivero 2001: 16) characterised by the 'intrusions of distant events into everyday consciousness' (Giddens 1991: 27). It has been made much clearer that it is in our own interest that Donald Trump wears a face mask!

Because the corona virus attacks each and every one of us, it is demanding that we become 'our brother's and sister's keeper'. The virus has put a spotlight on what Rawls (1971: 7) called the social justice system, i.e. 'the basic structures of society ….the way in which the major social institutions distribute fundamental rights and duties and determine the division of advantages from social cooperation'. The corona virus has highlighted the biases of our governance and social benefit systems and revealed much more clearly whom they protect and whom they neglect.

The challenges of the marginalisation of women and the youth that Mate highlights and those of migrants and refugees highlighted by Chilunjika and Masiiwa have been further exposed by COVID-19. In this volume, we have neglected the plight of the elderly, disabled and the sick. It is clear who bears most of the social cost of local and global development; this is being demonstrated at all levels of our societies. Reports on the impact of the corona virus have revealed very specific groups of people who have been disproportionately affected. In many places, it is showing how people are so marginalised and excluded that they cannot afford to follow the prescribed responses of social distancing, sanitising, washing hands and staying at home. What is assumed in national and global governance is just impossible to follow in many communities, because they have no water to wash hands, no homes to retreat to and no space to social distance. The United Nations (UN 2019) estimates that by 2050, 68% of the world population will be urbanised. 90% of this increase in population will be in Africa and Asia. Unless things change dramatically, the majority of this population will be moving into informal settlements.

Discovering the human in all of us

As globalisation processes push us towards the cosmopolitan ideal of global citizenship, they are helping us to discover more and more how all of us are human and intricately connected to each other and to our surrounding environments in ways that challenge the dominant assumptions about local and global social realities. Chigumira and Kwaramba drew our attention to the ecological challenges we face as we struggle to establish a balanced relationship with the environment that sustains human and other forms of life. This is an opportunity for all of us to re-learn to be human. Fundamentally, global phenomena like the COVID-19 pandemic, climate change and global financial crises are making it clearer that we are human beings in history, and that these global challenges are making a mockery of many of the ideologies and conceptual categories we have used to understand ourselves.

As Mbembe (2000) points out, this should be the end of monologues which make certain modes of self-writing obsolete. He urges us as Africans to grow '… the desire to break down barriers and open us to global and traverse questions, the same interest in deterritorialisation, the same rejection of localism and nativism and their blinding, intolerant effects, the same audacity in the choice of themes for discussion, the same diversity of approaches and the same fierceness of debate',

COVID-19 has demonstrated that it knows no political, economic or cultural boundaries. It has demonstrated the negative and sometimes dangerous politics of the social divisions and walls we have been building at national, regional and global levels. It is making a mockery of some of the policies on migration, refugees, citizenship, property rights, taxation and prisons. As Mills (2000: 15) declares in his old language, 'The history that now affects every (hu)man is world history'. Explaining why this may be so, Giddens (1991:2) says that 'The reorganisation of time and space, plus the dis-embedding mechanisms, radicalise and globalise pre-established institutional traits of modernity; and they act to transform the content and nature of day-to-day social life.' Held and Roger (2013: 4) explain how because of the global reorganisation of space and time and dis-embedding mechanisms,

> the interdependencies created by complex global processes, from the economic to the ecological, connect the fates of communities to each other across the world. Global interconnectedness means that emerging risks or policy failures generated in one part of the world can quickly travel across the globe to those that have had no hand in their generation.

This is an experience we can all attest to given what we have gone through with the COVID-19 pandemic, the global financial crisis and climate change. No amount of blame can help solve this challenge. This is our reality.

Because of globalisation, we have seen more and more global challenges that require global responses. This means that African struggles must become more global and connect to other struggles. This in turn means going beyond the mostly non-viable nation-states and their 'perforated sovereignties' (de Rivero 2001) and linking up to struggles that rely on global solidarity. This can be seen in the growth of the anti-globalisation movement aimed at protesting corporate-led globalisation with protest organised against the most powerful countries and economic powers of the world. We can learn a lot from the anti-globalisation struggles and the questions they are asking. We can learn a lot about how global industrial complex systems of domination recreate themselves and how, as global cosmopolitan citizens we can respond (Best et al. 2011). The following are some of the lessons that we can learn from the COVID-19 experience:

Discernment – Reading the signs of the times and widening the national and global social imaginary

The COVID-19 experience teaches us the importance of discernment. Discernment is a certain way of understanding and interpreting social reality as a moral social order. It is one that calls for a wide social imaginary that makes use of the best of available social analysis and the most mature and inclusive emotional response. It is what Mills (2000) called, in a rather narrow way, the 'sociological imagination' and Zygmunt Bauman (in Giddens 1991) called 'thinking sociologically'. But we know, and both sociologists knew, that it calls for more than the contribution of sociology. West (1993: 16) says that discernment demands 'the capacity to provide a broad and deep analytical grasp of the present in light of the past'. This must include a 'nuanced historical sense' that acknowledges the contributions of all civilisations and peoples and 'never losing sight of the humanity of others'. It is a broad sweep of human self-consciousness that recognises and appreciates how human personal lives are intricately linked to the broader structures and institutions of society and their histories and value systems.

COVID-19 is teaching us that science is important but not enough. Social sciences, on their own, are inadequate. We also need humanities and the arts and sport. As Mbembe (2000) has declared, '...let music, literature, and film mix with the social sciences! Let artists, writers, media, and researchers talk to each other!' We have seen all these professions and social, political and religious callings collaborate to respond to COVID-19, each in its unique way. As Zimbabweans we must learn the complexities of human struggles and acknowledge the efforts of everyone in these struggles.

We must admit that COVID-19 has clearly shown that issues of health care, poverty, employment and marginalisation are not merely 'private issues of milieu' (Mills 2000). It has highlighted the fact that we have a national system that is linked to a global system that has serious areas of weakness and neglect that can be analysed by looking at the various vulnerable groups that include older people, women, young workers, migrant households, unprotected workers, people living in shelters, people who are homeless or in informal settlements, and people with underlying health issues. The crisis has also deepened public concerns about racism, sexism, patriarchy, class and other social and economic inequalities.

COVID-19 has challenged what we imagine to be the universal. It has demonstrated how the marginalised, the forgotten and the exploited must be seen as part of the universal. It is very clear now that for as long as the virus exists somewhere, the rest of the country and indeed the world is not safe. It has highlighted what we already knew, that poverty is a threat to national and global peace and that inequality is expensive. In this way

COVID-19 is pushing to widen and deepen the imagination of the powerful in existing national and global governance.

Tools of analysis that hide rather than reveal the objects of analysis

COVID-19, just like the global financial crisis of 2008 and Cyclone Idai, caught everyone by surprise. They all exposed the weaknesses of our gaze and our self-understanding as a nation and as a global community. It has exposed a lot of lies we tell about the global economic and political situation. A lot of dust and ugly truths have come from under the carpet. In Shona, we say *'Rinemanyanga hariputirwe'* meaning 'you cannot wrap up and hide that which has horns'; the horns will pierce through your wrapping paper to expose what is underneath – corruption, unfairness and weak governance.

With hindsight and with better and more appropriate discernment, we should have seen it coming. In the context of the global financial crisis, the leading economists were using neo-liberal assumptions and mathematical models, and financial practitioners were so caught up in excitement of growth strategies that they failed to see the now obvious risks. In the context of the COVID-19 pandemic, we must learn that our global survival now depends on our attention to the weakest links rather than on supporting the strongest and loudest players.

Poverty, neglect, injustice and exploitation are becoming more of a danger to our global survival, just as unbridled economic growth, the exploitation of nature and the dumping of industrial waste is a danger to our environment and climate. We need to address these challenges directly – locally and globally. The market approach, with its assumptions of focusing on self-love and not benevolence, on private property and not the common good, will not work. We must widen our gaze to acknowledge nature and its reproductive capacities that form the foundations upon which our economies stand. We must also acknowledge the contributions of families and communities that continue to provide care and support even as they are relegated to the private sphere and suffer neglect and exploitation.

In looking to go beyond COVID-19 to the new normal, we need some minimum standards for national, regional and global engagement and practice. The standards must point to the possibility of establishing alternatives to the cultures of violence, neglect, exploitation and oppression that dominate us and that COVID-19 has exposed. They suggest values and principles that could act as guidelines for discovering new ways of doing things. Ideals and principles help to give us visions of what things could be like. They help us to go beyond how things are, as a matter of fact, especially if the present is full of injustices and evils. In this sense, the ethical social principles can be transformed into personal and social virtues that we can cultivate in ourselves and in our institutions in order to replace the systems of violence and neglect.

Re-discovering the common good

COVID-19 is making us re-discover the common good which is truly common. History has given us reasons to mistrust the common good. Americans and Europeans, Asians and Africans all have experiences of the common good being used by a few against the rest. But we are concretely discovering that the fact that the common good can be hijacked by a few does not mean we should give up on the idea. The fact that the democratic project has been limited should not make us give up on it.

Deciding on what is of value

The COVID-19 pandemic has raised questions about what the dominant economic and political paradigms place value on. We now can appreciate what feminists and real-life economists have been saying all along, that life and the environment supporting life has greatest priority. Even those who value the economy in the narrow sense of the word have to admit that we cannot imagine the economy without life but we can imagine the other way round. If this is correct, why then have we allowed our political and economic priorities to ignore and even destroy life and its environments? The COVID-19 pandemic is clearly a consequence of such neglect. Moving forward, national, regional and global governance must pay attention to what is of most value – our environments, families and communities.

In the history of humanity, there have of course been disagreements on the criteria for recognising what is of value in the global economy. Learning the history of major economic theories and how they account for value can help us to appreciate the blind spots of the dominant governance paradigms today. Ha-Joon Chang (2014: 451) argues about economics that:

> Economics is a political argument. It is not – and can never be – a science; there are no objective truths in economics that can be established independently of political, and frequently moral, judgements. Therefore, when faced with an economic argument,

you must ask the age-old question 'Cui bono?' (Who benefits?), first made famous by the Roman statesman and orator, Marcus Tullius Cicero.

The same can be argued about national and global governance after COVID-19. The pandemic has demonstrated that national and global governance can no longer be left to be monopolised by a few, whether experts or politicians. National and global governance is a political and moral system that tries, among other things, to answer the question 'Who benefits?' It is true that we have experienced collective vulnerability. And yet our vulnerabilities have not always been the same.

As pointed out in the Introduction, the contributions in this book point out the various windows of opportunity that the nation can take advantage of. These include the following:

1. Widening the national social imaginary and the accompanying moral and emotional responses in order to build the foundations of a new inclusive nation and heal the wounds of the past.
2. Encouraging an inclusive national development that addresses past injustices and inequalities, especially against women, young people and the environment.
3. Reaching out to all Zimbabweans in the country and those who have migrated all over the world and have been marginalised, impoverished, ignored and sometimes demonised in order to solicit their full participation in national development.
4. Re-engaging the international community in order to contribute to the building of a just and prosperous global economic, political, cultural and environmental system that is able to support and complement the aspiration of Zimbabwe's national development.

As we look ahead towards Zimbabwe at 50, it is our fervent collective hope that Zimbabwean society will draw from its rigorous introspection on the past 40 years, self-criticism, experiences and lessons in development, democracy and transformation. It will require collective and national commitment, solidarity, and vision as well as resilient optimism to make the next decade a better one. This will require innovative approaches to development and governance, national dialogue and social inclusion.

References

Best, S., R. Kahn, A.J. Nocella II and P. McLaren (eds) (2011) *The Global Industrial Complex: Systems of Domination*. Lanham, MD: Lexington Books.

Chang, H-J. (2014) *Economics: The User's Guide*. London: Penguin Books.

de Rivero, O. (2001) *The Myth of Development: The Non-Viable Economies of the 21st Century*. London: Zed Books.

Giddens, A. (1991) *Modernity and Self-Identity: Self and Society in the Late Modern* Age. Cambridge: Polity Press.

Held, D. and C. Roger (eds) (2013) *Global Governance at Risk*. Cambridge: Polity Press.

Kanyenze, G., T. Kondo, P. Chitambara and J. Martens (2011) *Beyond the Enclave: Towards a Pro-Poor and Inclusive Development Strategy for Zimbabwe*. Harare: Weaver Press.

Mbembe, A. (2000) 'The End of Monologues' and 'African Modes of Self-Writing', *CODESRIA Bulletin,* 1.

Mills, C.W. (2000) *The Sociological Imagination,* with a new Afterword by Todd Gitlin. Oxford: Oxford University Press.

Moyo, S. and P. Yeros, (eds), *Reclaiming the Land: The Resurgence of Rural Movements in Africa, Asia and Latin America*. London: Zed Books.

Pope Francis (2015) Speech at the Second World Meeting of Popular Movements at the Expo Feria Exhibition Centre, Santa Cruz de la Sierra, Bolivia, 9 July.

Rawls, J. (1971) *A Theory of Justice*. Oxford: Oxford University Press.

United Nations (UN) (2019) *World Urbanization Prospects: The 2018 Revision*. New York: United Nations Department of Economic and Social Affairs.

West, C. (1993) *Prophetic Thought in Postmodern Times*. Monroe, ME: Common Courage Press.

www.ingramcontent.com/pod-product-compliance
Lightning Source LLC
Chambersburg PA
CBHW071205240426
43668CB00032B/2098